"I'd love to see every math teacher take the kind of thoughtful and professional approach to their journey of learning that Chase Orton invites us to. Chase invites us to disrupt the status quo of professional development. He asks teachers to see past the top-down barriers and systemic constraints—politics, high-stakes tests, yo-yo administrative decisions, and all kinds of compliance and evaluation measures—to take charge of our own professional learning. Chase calls on us to see our practice through the eyes of our students, and at the same time to reflect on our practice and to collaborate with colleagues in genuine ways for mutual growth. Grounded in real stories of students' experiences and teachers' journeys, he offers concrete, interactive strategies teachers can use to continually move closer to being the teachers we want to be—those who are always focused on our goal of more and more effectively helping every one of our students become curious mathematical thinkers who embrace the power of mathematics and see themselves as 'math people.'"

Cathy Seeley
Mathematics Educator, Speaker, and Writer
Past President of the National Council of Teachers of Mathematics
McDade, TX

"As one of the most reflective, insightful, and thoughtful educators I've ever worked with in my 30 years of math education, Chase Orton delivers an emotive call to action for teachers to reclaim control over their professional growth. *The Imperfect and Unfinished Math Teacher* takes the most impactful components of lesson study and packages them in a way that accommodates the chaotic realities of day-to-day life as classroom teachers. Join Chase on a journey to empower yourself and each other by learning how to be active partners in each other's professional growth.

Mark Goldstein
Vice President, Curriculum and Instruction
Center for Mathematics and Teaching
Redondo Beach, CA

"The vast majority of teacher professional development doesn't make a lasting difference, and it's time for us to disrupt the status quo. *The Imperfect and Unfinished Math Teacher* empowers all math educators to take control of their professional learning by laying out what needs to change, why it's so important, and how to get started. If you and your colleagues are seeking a more fulfilling and rewarding approach to improving your teaching craft, this is the book for you."

Robert Kaplinsky
President of Grassroots Workshops
Long Beach, CA

"*The Unfinished and Imperfect Math Teacher* is a clarion call to disarming, dismantling, and disrupting the math classroom that is loud enough to compete with a stack of Marshall amplifiers at any rock concert. The title takes the historical narrative of mathematics-slow failure-and shines a warm and illuminating light on it, inviting a collective of a new generation of teachers to be messy humans dabbling in equally messy mathematics. Written with unflinching vulnerability, compassion, and love, this book allows all readers to find and share their courage of satisfying incompleteness with an infectious purpose and energy. Chase Orton's humble manifesto for a soulful examination of our inner voice and outer intentions is the inflection point math education has been yearning for decades."

Sunil Singh
Author of *Pi of Life: The Hidden Happiness of Mathematics* and
Math Recess: Playful Learning in an Age of Disruption

"What is your math story? Likewise, what are your students' math stories? Chase Orton, still an imperfect and unfinished teacher, will not answer these questions for you. Instead, he challenges you to take on a culture of professional development that helps you—and your colleagues—to "flourish" and to do so from your students' vantage point. For too long, PD is done to us and not for us, thus we come away feeling we will never get that precious time back. It's long overdue that we take back PD through deliberate practice and honest conversations. Chase guides us in this journey, promising us nothing unless we put in the work and give ourselves grace.

He asks of us what he asks of himself—to be unafraid, to be vulnerable, and to refuse to play the blame game in shaping the kind of PD that nourishes our teaching soul and sharpens our teaching craft. And for what? For our students to write their own math stories—those that are imperfect and unfinished—so they may continue to be curious and thoughtful as learners of mathematics beyond our classroom walls."

Fawn Nguyen
Math TOSA, Rio School District
Oxnard, CA

The Imperfect and Unfinished Math Teacher

The Imperfect and Unfinished Math Teacher

A Journey to Reclaim Our Professional Growth

Chase Orton *(And You!)*

Foreword by Steve Leinwand

CORWIN **Mathematics**

For information:

Corwin
A SAGE Company
2455 Teller Road
Thousand Oaks, California 91320
(800) 233–9936
www.corwin.com

SAGE Publications Ltd.
1 Oliver's Yard
55 City Road
London, EC1Y 1SP
United Kingdom

SAGE Publications India Pvt. Ltd.
B 1/I 1 Mohan Cooperative
Industrial Area
Mathura Road, New Delhi 110 044
India

SAGE Publications
Asia-Pacific Pte. Ltd.
18 Cross Street #10–10/11/12
China Square Central
Singapore 048423

President: Mike Soules
Associate Vice President and Editorial
    Director: Monica Eckman
Publisher: Erin Null
Editorial Assistant: Nyle De Leon
Content Development Editor:
    Jessica Vidal
Senior Editorial Assistant:
    Caroline Timmings
Production Editor: Astha Jaiswal
Copy Editor: Christina West
Typesetter: Integra
Proofreader: Jennifer Grubba
Indexer: Integra
Cover Designer: Janet Kiesel
Marketing Manager:
    Margaret O'Connor

ISBN: 9781071841525

Printed in Canada.

This book is printed on acid-free paper.

22 23 24 25 26 10 9 8 7 6 5 4 3 2 1

CONTENTS

PART 3 ● CHANGING OUR CULTURAL MATH STORY   127

online resources

To access the Campfire Gathering Facilitation Guide, visit the *The Imperfect and Unfinished Math Teacher* Free Resources tab on the Corwin website or visit: bit.ly/3o7bBzq.

FOREWORD

What a wonderfully provocative juxtaposition of "imperfect and unfinished" on the one hand, and "math" on the other that Chase Orton presents to us. In reality the mathematics—too often viewed and taught as perfect and finished—is more typically an imperfect learning trajectory with which all teachers of mathematics must wrestle. And the teaching—nearly always unfinished when we are honest with ourselves—continually evolves in our classrooms. This book challenges us to join an evolution of our professional journey that is built around reflection, recalibration, and collaboration.

Consider, as Chase does, the challenge of expecting an unattainable perfection—the reality of circuitous, and often scary, paths taken by every professional. The incessant self-questioning about: *How do I get better? How do I better serve my parents, administration, students? What conditions could support this improvement process? What do I need from others and what must I bootstrap for myself? How do we learn to accept the need to cut ourselves some slack, to dial back the pressure, and share the load?* These are all critical perspectives for becoming a healthier, happier, and more effective teacher of mathematics.

In this daring and compassionate book, Chase Orton takes us on a journey of professional growth as we strive for more equitable processes and outcomes. The book you are about to read is part roadmap, part guidebook, part memoir, and part powerful rallying cry for change. I hope you will absorb the compelling narrative, reflect on the questions and vignettes inserted throughout, and engage in the kinds of collaborative discussions that can further us all on our personal and professional journey of improvement. Welcome aboard!

Steve Leinwand
Fellow Math Change Agent

ACKNOWLEDGMENTS

The Imperfect and Unfinished Math Teacher reflects the culmination of what I've learned from my own classroom experiences and from hundreds of colleagues who've shared their personal stories over the years about their professional toils and triumphs in the math classroom. These pages represent what I've learned from others about *how we get better at the craft*—the technical art and the artful technique—of teaching mathematics to a classroom of students in ways that meet their myriad of needs. This book also represents what I've learned from others about *how we stay engaged and sustain our passion for our work* so that we want to keep improving our ability to grow students who are mathematically proficient and, just as important, mathematically curious and mathematically empowered.

I am here because of the colleagues, mentors, and students who have challenged me to grow and have helped me flourish in my career. If you know me, you have influenced my work, and I hope you see your wisdom and your brilliance reflected in the pages ahead. Thank you.

I would like to specifically acknowledge the following people: my loving family; my editor, Erin Null; my co-thinking partner, Jeff Crawford; Steve Leinwand; Shelli Wright; all my former students; Jim Bosman and my teachers at Souhegan High School in Amherst, New Hampshire; Frinde Maher and my professors at Wheaton College in Norton, Massachusetts; Wendy Welshans and my colleagues at the Forman School in Litchfield, Connecticut; Mohammed Elgazzar and Jimmy Frickey and my colleagues at the Eagle Rock School and Professional Development Center in Estes Park, Colorado; Mandy Breuer, Amy Frame, Phil Schwenk, and my colleagues at Environmental Charter High School in Lawndale, California; Mark Goldstein, Shelley Kriegler, and my colleagues at Center for Mathematics and Teaching; Lauren McCabe, John Matich, Paul Payne, and my colleagues at LA Education Partnership; Francisco Villegas, Joy Min, and my colleagues at the Partnership for LA Schools; my colleagues at Illustrative Mathematics; Dan Meyer and the amazing folks at Desmos; Cresta McIntosh; Sean True; Fawn Nguyen; Dave Hendry; Michael Farber; Robert Kaplinsky; Laruen Wilson; Javier Arechiga; Chrissy Newell; Joe Schwartz;

Mihai Banulescu, Infinity Ra El; and the other deep thinkers I met in the desert communities of Joshua Tree, California, and Kearny, Arizona; Anthony Diecidue (@artofant) and Hudson Haggett (@hudsa.doodle) for their artwork; and the hundreds of educators in the #MTBoS and #iteachmath communities on Twitter who have helped me grow over the years.

ABOUT THE AUTHOR

Chase Orton's unique career path has been guided by his passion for creating productive and inspired math classrooms that are engaging and fulfilling for both students and their teachers. After graduating from Wheaton College in Norton, Massachusetts, he embarked on a 12-year journey as a math teacher at three different schools: The Forman School in Litchfield, Connecticut; The Eagle Rock School and Professional Development Center in Estes Park, Colorado; and Environmental Charter High School in Lawndale, California. In 2012, Chase founded Mobius Educational Consulting and ventured out as an independent collaborator with different nonprofits and school districts in California. He's worked as an instructional coach for Los Angeles Education Partnership and the Partnership for Los Angeles Schools. He partnered with the Center for Mathematics and Teaching as lead author of *MathLinks*, a comprehensive middle school math curriculum. He is a Desmos Fellow and a Certified Facilitator for Illustrative Mathematics. As an accomplished facilitator of lesson study for K-12 math teachers, Chase currently invests his professional time partnering with districts that are interested in taking a teacher-centered, teacher-directed approach to professional development. *The Imperfect and Unfinished Math Teacher* is his first book. An aspiring storyteller, Chase lives on the road and is currently collecting stories from math teachers all over the country. Interested in having Chase come visit you? He would love to hear from you. You can follow Chase on Twitter (@mathgeek76) and online at www.chaseorton.com. He shares his stories from the road on Instagram (@TheTravelingStoop).

INTRODUCTION: GRACE AND THE ART OF NOT KNOWING

The great gate is wide open-and nobody is obstructing it.

—Alan Watts, *Waiting for Magic* (2020, 13:16)

A Book of Stories

This is a book of stories about being an imperfect and unfinished teacher of mathematics. Some of these stories are mine. Most of these stories are from the hundreds of teachers who've graciously let me be in their math classrooms over the years. All of these stories are true.

You are an author of this book—just the same as me—and I'm inviting you to share your story with us and the colleagues you work with. Even though you, like me, are imperfect and unfinished, we have much to learn from each other. And it's time we start thinking differently about the ways we relate to each other and how we talk about the work we do.

We will never be perfect teachers, not because we are incapable or incompetent. We are imperfect because there is simply so much we don't know—we can't know—when it comes to our work and meeting the needs of our students. We are always forced to do our best with the information and tools we have at the time. And we must perform our craft while navigating a professional schedule that never gives us the time we need to pause and reflect on our learning so we can calibrate and collaborate together on ways we can improve our efficacy.

The job of a teacher is to fill the gap between what students need and what the school system offers them. This has always been true about our role in society, but if you taught during the pandemic and navigated the world of remote learning, you know just how wide that gap can be. Never before in our lives had our students needed so much, and never before had the system of education been so overwhelmed. Routines and structures fell away. Long-standing traditions and cultural expressions were interrupted. Children vanished into the digital ether. Fewer faces. Fewer voices. Fewer laughs and smiles and smelly farts. Our entire mental model of not just what it means to be a teacher but what it means to be a human being was disrupted.

And what did teachers do in the face of these insurmountable obstacles? What we always do—we remained *unfinished* and filled that gap. We stretched our expertise, our love, our souls in ways we never thought possible. All of us, in our own unique ways, exercised our creative genius and expanded our potential and accomplished things we not only hadn't done before—we accomplished things we couldn't even imagine before.

Along the way, we also had a chance to reclaim an essential quality about our humanity, as we've been reminded how important it is to give more grace to our students, our colleagues, and most important, to ourselves. Grace is an essential tool in the Art of Not Knowing. And it will be a key component in our relationships together and how we position each other as collaborators in each other's professional growth.

Stories Help Us Test Our Beliefs and Question Our Actions

As we look at the years ahead, we are aware that much is uncertain, and we must continue to embrace a mindset of "not knowing" as we face the novel challenges to come. It's a lot of pressure being a teacher and embracing this "not knowing" mindset. We're teachers after all! We're supposed to have the answers, right? If you believe that to be true, I invite you to test that belief, because there is tremendous power and freedom in admitting to ourselves, and to each other, that much of what we think we know about effective math teaching may not be true. A "not knowing" mindset is a productive belief for furthering our teaching craft because we can begin to test our beliefs and question our actions. And when we practice the Art of Not Knowing in our classrooms, we position ourselves to share authority with our students because they see us as learners with them—instead of seeing us as someone who is holding all the answers.

I will continue to ask us to test some of our beliefs and question our actions as we strengthen our relationships with each other and establish a new culture of professionalism. But please know this: I'm no answer key. I'm a learner—a co-thinker—alongside you as we grow our craft.

Stories Share Authority and Position Us All as Capable Learners

I'm uncomfortable with the title of "author" because it implies that my lived experiences have authority over yours—and they don't. We are colleagues, you and I, and stories are my way of sharing authority with you. They are invitations for us to reflect together and share with each other the beliefs that we have about our professional identity and our teaching practice. When we listen *openly* and *intently* to the meaning others make from these stories, we begin to develop an appreciation for both what makes us unique and what connects us together.

These stories are not about being right or wrong—there are no right or wrong answers to many of the dilemmas we face in our career. These stories are opportunities to get to know ourselves and know each other a bit more deeply. With this lens in place, I offer you a story from my own career. I call it the Rudy Story.

The Rudy Story

Rudy was affable, humorous, and equipped with a charming smile. He was a young man who was outwardly curious by nature and always sought to help others. He was liked by everyone for his kind and genuine heart and his ability to lift spirits when he walked into the room. Rudy was a kid that my teaching heart couldn't help but root for.

Continued →

→ Continued

When I taught Rudy, he was a senior in my class, taking Algebra 2 for the second time after failing it in his junior year (with a different teacher). Rudy had not built many enduring understandings over the years. Up to that point, he had survived math class by treating mathematics like it was a series of tricks and a disconnected jumble of isolated skills that needed to be memorized. In the fall term, he crammed for tests, made use of extra help, and would retake exams—sometimes again, again, and again—until he earned a passing grade.

The spring term, however, was a different story for Rudy. As the demands of his senior project and other coursework mounted, he fell further and further behind in math class. The consequences of failing were significant. All graduates from Rudy's charter school had to be "college eligible," and in California, that meant earning a passing grade in Algebra 2 to complete his "A-G requirements." Failure meant that Rudy would not walk at graduation, his pathway to a diploma would be extended into the summer, and he risked letting down his family's hopes (and his own) that he would be the first to go to college and earn a degree.

A lot of people's dreams were riding on Rudy's shoulders.

With about three weeks left of school, Rudy started to seek out extra help most days. He practiced problems enough that he was able to get right answers on the most basic and routine problems from some of the unit tests he had failed. He completed his financial literacy project on exponential functions. But despite his efforts, the deadline for senior grades came and went, and he still hadn't shown enough understanding of some of the core content on logarithms and polynomials.

Time had run out for Rudy and me. Now what happens?

WHAT WOULD YOU DO?

FOCUS

We will come back to the Rudy Story in a few chapters. Before moving forward, take a moment and put yourself in my shoes, standing there face-to-face with Rudy. Remember, there are no right or wrong answers here.

What would you do? Would you pass him and let him graduate? Would you give him an F? Figure out another option?

More important, *why* would you do that? What issues are most important to you about this moment? ●

Two Opposing and Unproductive Models of Professional Development

> Professional development is underperforming. It is neither professional, nor does it develop.
>
> —Leinwand (2019)

Our journey will require us to test some of our cultural beliefs about professional development and what we need as professionals seeking to improve our teaching craft. Currently, there are two opposing—and unproductive—beliefs that dominate much of our culture of professional development as math teachers.

On the one hand, effective math teaching is viewed as an innate gift, something we're bestowed with at birth. In this model of professional development, we are given our textbooks and our technology and then left alone in our classrooms to figure it all out. The space of our professional learning becomes siloed away from our space of professional practice and a culture of isolationism forms. And in this culture, teaching becomes a very private act.

Believing in the "teaching gift" also creates a culture where our ability to teach mathematics effectively is viewed as being "fixed"—it is something that "veteran" teachers can't learn if they haven't already. I hear this sentiment a lot from administrators: *What we need to do is find new teachers—teachers who get kids these days. If we just find the right teachers, things will get better.* Rubbish. We don't have a problem with finding the right teachers—*we are the right teachers.* But we're put in a position where we're not given what a professional needs to grow their craft.

On the opposing side, there's a model of professional development that seeks to reduce effective teaching down to a recipe—a checklist of "best practices" that can be marked on an observation form. I also hear this sentiment a lot from administrators: *Research says this is what "equitable instruction" looks like in the math classroom. If we can hold our teachers accountable for these actions, then we know we are achieving equity and meeting the needs of our students.* Also rubbish. Checklists are easy tools to use in a top-down approach to education reform, but they are often not productive feedback for us as teachers. They only tell us if we're compliant—not if we're effective or how we can get better.

FURTHER LEARNING

The Teaching Gap by James Stigler and James Hiebert and *Building a Better Teacher* by Elizabeth Green explain these opposing approaches and why they are ineffective.

To be clear, both of these beliefs are as *untrue* as they are *unproductive* to our professional growth. Effective math teaching is not an innate gift. There is no "teaching gene" that enables some of us to "get kids" or "get math" better than others. Nor can effective math teaching be reduced to a recipe that anyone can follow. The art of teaching is too complex—and too personal—to be measured by a checklist on a clipboard during a 10-minute walkthrough.

Effective Math Teaching Is a Craft Worthy of Study

Neither accountability nor autonomy is enough ... because both arguments subscribe to the myth of the natural-born teacher. In both cases, the assumption is that good teachers know what to do to help their students learn. These good teachers should either be allowed to do their jobs or be held accountable for not doing them, and they will perform better. Both arguments ... rest on a feeble bet: that the average teacher will figure out how to become an expert teacher—alone.

—Green, *Building a Better Teacher* (2014, p. 13)

Teaching is a craft, and like any craft, it is worthy of study. In fact, study is *necessary*. I do not mean simply academic study—we have enough academic research out there already. Perhaps too much. The study I'm referring to is in the more traditional, human-to-human sense because teaching is a cultural activity—it is something we learn best through each other. I'm inviting us to learn like all other professionals engaged in performing a complex skill—by watching each other perform the skill and reflecting together on what we see.

These Colleagues Are Watching Each Other Teach for the First Time

Claudine: *You know, Wendy, we've been teaching next to each other for three years, and this is the first time I'm going to see you teach mathematics.*

Claudine, Wendy, and I are about to walk into Claudine's second grade classroom. We spent the previous day sitting in a room together talking about different ways to get students to share their thinking more in math class. We crafted a lesson that we think will allow all students to help elevate their voice more *because that's what these teachers value the most right now*. We're going to observe Claudine's students first, then reflect, make some changes to the lesson, and then try again later today in Wendy's class. Despite spending the previous day together, this is news to me. I figured they'd have seen each other teach mathematics at some point, right? Even accidentally? Nope.

Claudine: *Yeah, it feels kinda weird, right?*

Me: *When's the last time you saw someone teach a math lesson?*

Wendy: *A whole lesson? Jeez. I can't remember. Maybe not since I was student-teaching 15 years ago.*

Me: *Well, this is my first time teaching second graders. So there's a first time for everyone today, I guess.*

Claudine: *I wonder what we'll see.*

Wendy: *I bet we've missed out on seeing a lot.*

Experts in almost any field learn by watching their peers perform—doctors, welders, musicians, athletes, carpenters, artists, pilots, chess players, the list goes on. It is an inherent part of their culture of professionalism. We don't have that as teachers—yet. Routine, informal peer-to-peer observations of each other doing our craft is a foreign thing for many of us. But it needs to become a natural and familiar part of our culture of professionalism because becoming an expert math teacher requires us to go through our colleagues' classroom doors.

> *Experts in almost any field learn by watching their peers perform—doctors, welders, musicians, athletes, carpenters, artists, pilots, chess players, the list goes on. It is an inherent part of their culture of professionalism. We don't have that as teachers—yet.*

Now, you might be asking yourself: *Did he just say we need to go into each other's classrooms?* Yes. Yes, I did.

Perhaps the strongest headwind working against our professional growth as teachers—especially as teachers of mathematics—is the fact that we work in a system that promotes isolation. The siloing effect of school structures and our teaching schedules normalize the professional act of teaching as a private practice conducted alone behind our closed classroom doors. As a result, we often find ourselves without the necessary relationships we need to talk *authentically* about our struggles with each other, let alone open our classroom doors and risk failing in front of each other.

We will talk quite a bit about relationships in this book because we need to replace our current culture of professional isolationism with a culture of professional collaboration where we have the trust and understanding we need to be productive partners in each other's professional growth. If you're hesitant about being in a colleague's classroom—or if you're anxious about having colleagues in yours—you're not alone. At first, we might feel insecure, maybe even a twinge of shame, revealing to each other what is going on in our math classrooms. But I assure you, math class didn't work for all of my students, and it's not working for all your colleagues' students either. Each and every one of us is bothered by the same universal truth: *our teaching expertise is falling short of achieving the productive and equitable outcomes we desire for our students.*

> *Each and every one of us is bothered by the same universal truth: our teaching expertise is falling short of achieving the productive and equitable outcomes we desire for our students.*

This Book in a Paragraph

I've written this book because I believe we must learn how to create a more equitable, inclusive, and cohesive culture of professionalism *for ourselves.* We have more than 40 years of evidence that suggests the system won't do it for us. *The Imperfect and Unfinished Math Teacher* is an invitation to all K-12 teachers of mathematics to join in a grassroots movement to disrupt the status quo of our current structure of professional development from the "inside-out" so that we can create the culture of professionalism we need to improve our teaching expertise. This book is a map that you and your colleagues can use to cultivate the empowering culture of professionalism you need to achieve more productive, equitable, *and joyful* outcomes in your classrooms for both you and your students. Implementing the beliefs and actions in this book will position us to become more active partners in each other's professional growth so that we can navigate the obstacles on our professional landscape with renewed focus and a greater sense of individual and collective efficacy.

PART 1

AN INVITATION TO A JOURNEY

THE NEED FOR A NEW CULTURE OF PROFESSIONALISM

The real voyage of discovery consists not in seeking new landscapes, but in having new eyes.

—Marcel Proust (1923/2003)

Learning to See With New Eyes

I'm inviting you to embark on a journey with me—a voyage of discovery, as Proust might call it—where our purpose is to develop "new eyes" about how we grow as professionals who teach mathematics to young people. Because we are social beings and learn best through other people, I invite you to consider asking other colleagues to take this journey with us. To understand why we need to take this journey, and why we must take it *together*, we start with Brenda and her math story.

CONNECT TO YOUR OWN STORY

FOCUS

As you read, I invite you to think about the math stories you've heard from others over the years about their school experiences in math class.

How does Brenda's math story compare?

How do you feel when someone tells you they aren't a "math person"? ☾

Brenda's Math Story

Brenda is telling me about her work as a chef. We've just met, and I can tell from her body language that she's passionate about what she does. She's leaning forward and gestures openly as she talks. She has me interested, engaged. When she asks what I do, I hesitate for a quick moment. This moment in social conversation is a pivotal one that I often face as a high school math teacher. Once people find out what I do, any established rapport suddenly becomes threatened. Some folks are enthused about my work, but far too many have the same reaction as Brenda. There's a noticeable shift in the energy of the conversation. The body language becomes more guarded as they lean back, expressing a troubled, sometimes even pained, emotion on their face—just as Brenda is doing now.

I am not a math person.

Her tone sounds almost apologetic, as if she's embarrassed to share this news. I assure her that she is not alone. I have heard others say this many times before over the years. Perhaps you have too. When I ask her why she believes this about herself, she begins to tell me her math story ...

I always got good grades in math. But I didn't always understand it. I was just good at school in general and had a knack for memorizing math facts and the steps for getting the right answers. Because of my grades, I was recommended for honors level math in eighth grade. I remember the teacher would set up competitions in class. He would put us in groups and see who could get the answers the fastest and awarded points for both speed and accuracy. I couldn't work as fast as the others in my group. The pressure made me forget everything. I began to hate class. My group never did well, and I felt stupid because I didn't get math as quickly as my classmates did.

In high school, it just got worse. I remember getting sick my junior year and missing two weeks of school. I was already way behind, and

Continued →

→ Continued

> *when I came back nothing made sense in math class. I would break down and cry at least once a week. I remember the teacher trying to comfort me and said "Don't beat yourself up. Everyone has their limit in math. Maybe this is yours." I guess I thought that was true, because I never took another math class again. I wanted to be done with it forever.*
>
> She pauses as if there's more to say. I interpret the moment as a good opportunity to be quiet and hold space for it.
>
> *And it hasn't bothered me until recently. My daughter, Page, is in seventh grade now, and I get anxious when I help her with her homework. She's falling behind. Because of her low test scores, she has to go to intervention after school and she feels dumb. I just don't want her to end up like me, hating math. I want her to feel empowered in the challenges she's going to face. But I don't know how to help her.*

Oof. Here's a capable and talented woman with a successful career as a chef—a career that requires a significant degree of mathematical reasoning—who doubts her ability to reason through mathematics that her 13-year-old daughter is being asked to learn in middle school. Guilt and shame tug at her deeply. Like any parent, she wants her child to be successful in mathematics. And she's worried that because she doesn't consider herself a math person, she's going to limit her daughter's potential.

Our Cultural Math Story

We all have a math story. While Brenda's math story is unique to her, it is not uncommon to many Americans who have their own unproductive perspective on mathematics and their own math identity. Most folks don't like math. Much of the anecdotal data we read on social media and hear in real life tells a story of dwindling interest in mathematics combined with an almost contagious distaste for it. It's a subject that often stirs emotions of disdain or resentment—or worse, memories of trauma from their experience in math class. And a discouraging number of people don't have productive math stories because their learning needs—whether emotional, social, cognitive, or otherwise—weren't met in the math classroom. At some point in their schooling, they, like Brenda, decided that math wasn't for them.

Math Story
A math story describes a person's relationship with mathematics. It is how they describe their math identity and how they exercise their sense of mathematical agency.

I've grown quite disheartened by our cultural math story. As my colleague, I imagine you might feel similarly too. It seems so unnecessary, doesn't it? Why haven't we, as a society, been able to do a better job of creating citizens who have a positive and empowered relationship with mathematics?

> Why haven't we, as a society, been able to do a better job of creating citizens who have a positive and empowered relationship with mathematics?

It's certainly not for a lack of effort from teachers of mathematics. As professionals who care for the well-being of all our students, we are striving for more productive and equitable outcomes in our classrooms. We want to help our students author a productive and *unfinished* math story—a belief that they can continue to learn mathematics conceptually, improve their fluency of mathematical skills, and find joy in solving mathematical problems. But despite our best efforts over the past decades, too many of our former students left math class without a positive math identity and a fostered sense of math agency. Some, like Brenda, left feeling marginalized, disconnected, and barred from further entry.

LANGUAGE NOTE

Like the authors of *Principles to Action*, I use the labels "productive/unproductive" to describe many of our beliefs and actions because they are less pejorative and divisive compared to words like "good/bad" and "right/wrong."

Steering Clear of the Blame Game: Hard on Systems, Soft on People

I want to be very clear that our journey together requires us to be critical of the system we work in without being critical of the people we work with. I'm not blaming you or anyone else for our cultural math story.

Our current cultural math story is unintentional—no one in the education system wants to rob students of their mathematical identity and agency. But the truth is—at all levels of math education—math class still isn't working for many of our students. Opportunity gaps persist, especially for Black and Latinx students and students from marginalized and impoverished communities. Our cultural math story is the natural and unavoidable outcome of decades of policies in math education that have, for the most part, been unproductive toward improving the teaching and learning for all students in math classes.

In order to change our cultural math story, we must have the courage to ask ourselves some uncomfortable questions—and to be able to answer them without implying fault or insinuating blame. With this lens in place, I ask the following:

➤ With what we know from research about how students learn mathematics, why are a sizable portion of students still having unproductive, unsuccessful, or even unhealthy experiences in math class?

➤ With what we know about productive, equitable teaching practices, why does teaching expertise continue to fall short of closing the inequitable achievement gaps we are witnessing in our math classrooms?

➤ In a nutshell, why is math class still not working for too many students?

You don't need me to tell you that our professional landscape is filled with insurmountable obstacles that work against our ability to meet the myriad of learning needs our students bring into our classrooms every day. Setting aside the massive impact of the socioeconomic inequalities we see in the demographics of our students, we continually have to navigate outlandish class sizes, tolerate draconian budgets, and use adopted textbooks that seem to suck the joy out of learning—and teaching—mathematics. The politics of grades, standardized tests, report cards, teacher evaluations, and school improvement plans—all the top-down systemic measures of accountability and compliance—continue to drag our focus away from what matters to us most: enhancing the mathematical identity of our students in ways that foster their sense of agency as mathematical thinkers.

Steering clear and avoiding the blame game means focusing our attention away from these "Immovable Mountains"—the obstacles within our professional landscape that impede our efforts to achieve productive and equitable outcomes, but that are beyond our influence to change as classroom teachers. It is unproductive to blame these Immovable Mountains because, when we do, we voluntarily surrender our sense of agency. Blaming our colleagues, ourselves, or any other individuals in the system is *extremely* unproductive because it robs us of our sense of individual or collective efficacy. Focusing on blame causes people to shut down, put up defensive walls, and disconnect from others.

Immovable Mountains
the obstacles within our professional landscape that impede our efforts to achieve productive and equitable outcomes, but that are beyond our influence to change as classroom teachers.

Instead, we need to focus on the area of our landscape that we can influence the most—our own professional learning—because one of the major reasons class still isn't working for so many math students *is because professional development still isn't working for so many math teachers.*

Professional Development Is Neither Professional Nor Does It Develop

The current structure of professional development often stands as an obstacle to the development of a culture of professionalism. Teachers frequently feel as though professional development is something done to them, instead of something done for them, involving them as active partners in their own professional growth. Too much of what currently is offered to teachers as professional development has limited value and makes little impact on their pedagogical knowledge, their practice, or their students' achievement.

—NCTM, *Principles to Action: Ensuring Mathematical Success for All*
(2014, p. 101)

What we call "professional development" (PD) is underperforming—and has for many years—*because it operates in a culture of professionalism that lacks equity.* When we look at our current system of PD through an equity lens, we can begin to see why.

Decades of top-down reform efforts to improve the outcomes in our math classrooms have created a system of PD that diminishes our sense of agency because it continually positions us as passive consumers rather than competent producers of our professional knowledge. And despite several decades of research that suggests how PD needs to be improved for math teachers, we continue to face a *cultural* "PD Gap"—a disconnect between the *culture* of PD we have and the *culture* of PD we need. We want more of our students to have productive math stories, but everywhere we look, we find ourselves stuck in a system of professional development that doesn't empower us to do that.

The Beacons: The Guiding Principles for Our Culture of Professionalism

> The hard work of improving teaching in the United States can't succeed without changes in the culture of teacher learning.
>
> —Stigler and Hiebert, "Closing the Teaching Gap" (1999, p. 32)

Creating a new culture of professionalism will require us to think very differently about how we currently perceive ourselves as professional learners and how professional growth can be achieved. The framework laid out in the opening chapters of this book will take some time to wrap your head around because I am asking you to develop a new way of thinking—a new mental model—about what teacher-centered, teacher-directed culture of professional learning can look like.

These Beacons describe the productive beliefs and actions that will serve as the guiding principles on our journey to creating our culture of professionalism.

Beacon 1: Our efforts to transform must come from the "inside-out."

It's up to us—the teachers of mathematics—to create the conditions we need to improve our teaching craft. We must be the agents of our own professional culture and learn how to foster each other's sense of agency by positioning ourselves and each other as capable producers of each other's professional knowledge. This is the culture of professionalism necessary for us to improve our teaching expertise in ways that lead to more productive and equitable student outcomes in our classrooms.

Beacon 2: Motivation is fostered most when we calibrate our measures to our values.

Much of our current PD focuses on improving assessment data. But our teaching souls are nourished more by the *human* data students give us—data that tells us that they are enjoying math class. I mean, that's what we really value, right? Seeing our students happy and engaged in learning mathematics with each other and authoring productive math stories? If so, then we need to learn how to enhance our professional identities by helping each other measure the things we truly value most as educators.

Beacon 3: We must continue to seek vantage, particularly from the students' perspective.

Because the choices we make in our teaching practice affect the math stories our students are generating, it's essential that we know how our students perceive our actions. We need to be in tune with their experience in math class by continuing to see the teaching and learning of mathematics from a vantage point in each other's classrooms. Sometimes we are not aware when our practices do not align with our purpose. Learning how to see math class from the students' perspective helps us check to see if what we believe is true and what we're doing is productive.

Beacon 4: Effective math teaching is a craft we can study best through each other.

As explained in the Introduction, Beacon 4 reminds us that we must leave the silos of our own classroom. The journey to furthering your teaching expertise goes through your colleague's classroom door.

Our Journey Is a Disruptive Act

> Serving students well is an act of critical resistance. It is political. And therefore it will not yield the normal rewards provided when we are simply perpetuating the status quo... . Teachers who care, who serve their students, are usually at odds with the environments wherein they teach. More often than not, we work in institutions where knowledge has been structured to reinforce dominator culture.
>
> —hooks, *Teaching Community: A Pedagogy of Hope* (2013, pp. 90-91)

To be clear, the Beacons are an invitation to be *disruptive*. They ask us to disrupt the homeostasis of the status quo of a PD system that doesn't serve us, or our students, well. These teacher-centered principles stand in direct opposition to our current top-down culture of professionalism, and embracing them on our journey will mean going against the dominant culture and challenging the dominant narratives that structure and influence our professional landscape in unproductive ways. In other words, our journey won't be easy. We can't go it alone. We're going to need each other. That's why we're taking this journey together.

Is This Journey for You?

I don't pretend to know what is unique about you, your teaching, your students, or your classrooms, but I believe this journey is for you because I think we are all craving the same thing: the rewarding sense of accomplishment we feel when we are able to achieve better outcomes in our math classes. And we're all facing the same obstacles to achieving that goal: the PD Gap. If what I have said so far resonates with you, if you're dissatisfied with the way PD is structured and you're wanting to take more control over how you grow your skills as a math teacher—and more control over your *teaching legacy* and the math stories you are helping to create—then I hope you consider joining the other teachers of mathematics who are taking this journey.

I firmly believe that we—the teachers of mathematics—hold the keys to meaningful reform in math education. We can change the cultural story of mathematics in this country if we learn how to change our professional story as teachers.

> ## KEY TAKEAWAYS FROM CHAPTER 1
>
> ✳ One reason math class isn't working for our students is because PD isn't working for math teachers. We continue to face a cultural "PD Gap"—a disconnect between the culture of PD we have and the culture of PD we need.
>
> ✳ The Beacons describe our guiding principles as we learn to cultivate a culture of professionalism for ourselves. We need to build trusting, mentoring relationships because the journey to becoming an expert math teacher goes through your colleague's classroom door.
>
> ✳ The ultimate purpose of our journey is to change our cultural relationship with mathematics by ensuring that more of our students author a productive and unfinished math story in our math classrooms.

INTERLUDE 1:
MORE DETAILS ABOUT
THE JOURNEY AHEAD

At the end of each chapter, there will be an "interlude"—a purposeful pause on our journey so we can deliberately reflect, calibrate, and collaborate on our learning together. Future interludes will contain specific actions and activities that you and your colleagues can take to build your culture of professionalism and develop the skills you will need to expand your teaching expertise.

At this juncture, I anticipate you might have some questions because the Beacons ask us to test some deeply held, long-standing cultural beliefs about what we need to improve our craft of teaching mathematics. I know our professional landscapes vary quite a bit. The day-to-day life of a third-grade teacher, an Algebra 2 teacher, and a special education teacher are very different. Because I want our journey to be as *accessible* and as *inclusive* as possible for any K-12 teacher of mathematics regardless of school setting, teaching experience, and current staff culture, Interlude 1 contains more details about this book and addresses some questions I hear from teachers as they start this journey.

Mission and Vision

The mission of *The Imperfect and Unfinished Math Teacher* is to change our cultural relationship with mathematics by creating a culture of professionalism where math teachers are agents in each other's professional growth and by collaboratively furthering each other's teaching expertise.

As more teachers of mathematics continue to join us on this journey, we will accomplish the threefold vision for this book:

1. We will establish a culture of professional learning in which all math teachers—regardless of their experience, background, or professional context—*embody a nourished sense of individual professional efficacy* as we pursue a flourishing practice of achieving more productive and equitable outcomes in our classrooms.
2. We will identify as part of a larger professional grassroots movement to *revitalize our work of improving our collective craft of teaching mathematics* by challenging the status quo of our current structure of professional development and learn how to become more active partners in each other's professional growth.
3. By improving the effectiveness of math teaching and the quality of student learning experiences in the classroom, *we will change our cultural "math story"* from one where many citizens identify as "not a math person" to one where all citizens identify as mathematically capable, mathematically confident, and, perhaps most important, mathematically curious.

RELATIONSHIPS

DELIBERATE PRACTICE

FOCUS   VANTAGE

Vantage
A position that offers
a strategic viewpoint
on something.

Outline of This Book

Part 1 of this book is an invitation to a journey to create a new culture of professionalism. In Chapter 2, we will define flourishment—the mindset necessary for our journey. In Chapter 3, we will learn about the Core Elements of Deliberate Practice—focus, vantage, and relationships. These Elements will structure our learning throughout this book as we take actions to expand our teaching potential and sustain our sense of professional vitality individually and collectively.

In Part 2, you will use the Core Elements of Deliberate Practice to develop your new culture of professionalism. These chapters contain stories that will help us get to know each other and are sequenced in a way to scaffold your progress toward fostering this culture with each other. Building culture and trusting relationships can sometimes happen quite quickly, but it should never be rushed. While there is no pacing plan for this journey, teachers generally complete the activities in Part 2 in about 6-8 weeks.

In Part 3, with our new culture of professionalism in place, we will test some of our beliefs about our professional identity, the curriculum we use, and how we assess our students. Using the Eight Mathematics Teaching Practices outlined by NCTM (Figure 1.1) in *Principles to Action* as a lens, we will question some of the actions by examining them from the students' perspective and discuss how they affect the math stories they are authoring. As we continue to strengthen our culture of professionalism, we will use the Core Elements of Deliberate Practice to reflect, calibrate, and collaborate in ways that will further our instructional expertise in the classroom.

Last, this book is a guide for using Core Elements of Deliberate Practice—focus, vantage, and relationships—to improve *any* aspect of your instructional craft as a math teacher. This makes *The Imperfect and Unfinished Math Teacher*

 NCTM's Eight Mathematics Teaching Practices

1. Establish mathematics goals to focus learning.
2. Implement tasks that promote reasoning and problem solving.
3. Use and connect mathematical representations.
4. Facilitate meaningful mathematical discourse.
5. Pose purposeful questions.
6. Build procedural fluency from conceptual understanding.
7. Support productive struggle in learning mathematics.
8. Elicit and use evidence of student thinking.

—NCTM, *Principles to Action: Ensuring Mathematical Success for All*
(2014, p. 10)

a useful companion to many of the other books on effective math teaching. Perhaps this book even encourages you to see the books in your current professional library with new eyes. What new learning could be gleaned from them now that you're equipped with these new tools?

Frequently Asked Questions

Q: When will I find time to make this journey?

A: The speed at which you take this journey is up to you and your colleagues. If you can carve out a few hours a month, you can reap the nourishing benefits of this work. I've discovered that once teachers start this journey, they find the work so transformative that they're compelled to keep going and look for strategic ways to embed this work into their busy schedules because they want to keep feeling the nourishing benefits of their improved expertise.

Q: Can I take this journey with teachers who don't teach my grade level or teach different high school content?

A: Yes! In fact, it's encouraged. There is substantial learning potential for us when we're in math classrooms that are less like our own.

Q: How will I schedule coverage to observe other classrooms?

A: Finding pupil-free time in your day to observe the teaching and learning in a colleague's classroom can be a challenge. If you work on a period schedule (like most middle and high school teachers), you hopefully have a "conference period" in your schedule that allows you the flexibility to step into each other's classrooms. If you don't work on a period schedule (like most elementary school teachers) or if you all have the same conference period as a department, you will need to find coverage for your own students while you observe.

Here are a few scheduling tricks I've seen teachers and site leaders use to find coverage:

- Elementary teachers strategically coordinate their math teaching time in their day with their colleagues a few times a month. They find coverage from a coach or principal during independent reading time (or something similar that can be supervised without any preparation) for their own students. When scheduled regularly at the same time every week, this routine usually works quite well.

- If you have the same conference period as your colleagues, you will need to think of moments in your teaching where coverage could happen. What might be some lessons that a coach, principal, or substitute could cover for you that wouldn't negatively affect the flow of learning in your own classroom? Some school sites dedicate some of the PD budget to pay for a substitute teacher to come in once or more a month. The substitute rotates through the day allowing each teacher an opportunity to observe a full lesson. Perhaps this is an avenue to explore with your leadership team.

Q: What if I'm the only one reading this on my staff?

A: This book works best if you are able to build relationships with your colleagues on site. Instead of reading it alone, consider inviting a coworker to join you on this journey. If you can't, then consider asking a colleague you know from a different school. Online meeting platforms can allow you to engage in the reflective parts of this book remotely. If you can't find someone and you want to read this book with others, we got you! Reach out to me by Twitter or email, and we'll connect you with other teachers doing this work.

If you're the only person on your site who is reading this book, you will need to talk with your colleagues about being in their classrooms and observing the teaching and learning of mathematics. If you're feeling hesitant about having the conversation (or you think they may be hesitant), consider the following as a way to start the dialogue:

> I'm reading this book to help me grow as a teacher. As a part of my learning, I'm encouraged to observe students in other math class-rooms to help me reflect and think about my own teaching practice with my own students. It would really help me grow as a teacher if I could observe your classroom a few times a month. How do you feel about that? What might make the process comfortable for you? What questions might you have?

And who knows? Maybe they'll want to read this book after they see how much you're growing. Win-win!

Q: What makes this a book for teachers of mathematics, specifically?

A: The research that forms the backbone of this book can be found in NCTM's (2014) *Principles to Action: Ensuring Mathematical Success for All* and their *Catalyzing Change Series*, a collection of three books—one each for elementary, middle, and high school educators—intended to initiate critical conversations on policies, practices, and issues that affect equity in the math classroom.

My lived professional experience for my entire career has been in *math* classrooms—12 years as a high school math teacher and another decade (and counting) as someone who facilitates professional learning for K-12 teachers of mathematics. I simply can't speak with much authority or create authentic stories for teachers of other subjects.

That said, every teacher, regardless of what they teach, can further their teaching expertise using the Core Elements of Deliberate Practice. Perhaps, this book inspires you to write *The Imperfect and Unfinished _____ Teacher* for teachers of other subjects. (That'd be awesome, huh? I'll even help you write it.) And as we will see in Chapter 3, the skills I'm offering you here will improve your performance at almost *anything*. Consider it an unexpected added value to this book!

NOTES

_____

_____

_____

_____

_____

_____

_____

_____

_____

_____

_____

_____

_____

_____

_____

_____

2

PROFESSIONAL FLOURISHMENT

Where We've Been

In Chapter 1, you were invited to embark on a journey to see our professional landscape with new eyes so that we can become more active partners in each other's professional growth.

Where We're Going

In Chapter 2, we will explore the concept of flourishment—the necessary mindset for our journey. We will be introduced to the Headwinds—the systemic forces that erode our sense of flourishment—and to the Beacons—the guiding principles that will help us grow and sustain our sense of flourishment.

I am a teacher at heart, and there are moments in the classroom when I can hardly hold the joy ... [and] teaching is the finest work I know. But at other moments, the classroom is so lifeless or painful or confused—and I am so powerless to do anything about it—that my claim to be a teacher seems a transparent sham.

—Parker Palmer, *Courage to Teach* (2017, p. 1)

A Window

Amanda, Alex, and LeRon want their math class to be a more productive learning experience for more of their students. They are, in their own uniquely personal ways, striving to achieve their vision of what productive, equitable learning should look, sound, and feel like in their math classrooms. And they are troubled by the human data that tells them their expertise is falling short. They see students authoring undesirable and unproductive math stories about themselves in their math class. And they're more than a little discouraged about it.

CONNECT TO YOUR OWN STORY

FOCUS

As you read, I invite you to ask yourself:

In what ways are these stories a window into your own teaching experiences?

What resonates with you about their professional dilemmas? How are your dilemmas unique to you? ●

Amanda, Alex, and LeRon

How do I get all my math students moving forward when they're all in different places academically? If I move forward, what will happen to my students who still don't get it? Will they ever catch up? But if we don't move forward, I won't cover all that I need to teach them. And I feel like I'm holding some of my students back. Every year I try something different, but every year some of my kids fall more behind and some of my kids aren't challenged enough.

—Amanda, fourth grade, 10th year of teaching

I want my students to be independent thinkers who can persevere through problems on their own and in groups. For most of my students, I can make learning rich with perplexity and wonder in a way that students want to learn mathematics—and are willing to work through their struggles and their mistakes. But for some of my students, I feel like I'm doing all the thinking for them—like I'm dragging them along to a solution they don't understand, let alone care about. I don't want to build a sense of learned helplessness for any of them, but I don't know what else I can do to support some of my students. I can't get them to do real work, but I also can't just sit there and watch them fail.

—Alex, ninth grade, second year of teaching

Continued →

→ Continued

> For me, teaching is all about relationships with my students. I can't teach a kid I don't know. I want each of them to feel seen, heard, and valued every day when they come into my classroom. I don't want my students to be able to hide, to let themselves be overlooked, but I feel that some of them are falling through the cracks anyway. It makes me sad to see them quit on themselves. When I press on some of them, they either shut down more or become disruptive and combative. I don't want to give up on them, but no matter what, every year, I'm not able to build the rapport I need to get some of my students to work with me and not against me.
>
> —LeRon, seventh grade, 26th year of teaching

Building Equity for Ourselves by Looking Through Windows

Brenda's math story from Chapter 1 and the stories above are opportunities to look through windows to see things that are *universally true for all of us and uniquely true to each of us*. We can empathize with Brenda because we all have a math story. Each of us went through a decade or more of math classes and formed our unique math identity along the way. (I will share my math story in Chapter 5.) And we can empathize with Amanda, Alex, and LeRon who are striving to achieve more equity in their classrooms because we are also striving to make math class successful for more of our students. And because teaching is such a personal craft and an expression of our identity, we all are striving to achieve equity in our own unique ways.

> Because teaching is such a personal craft and an expression of our identity, we all are striving to achieve equity in our own unique ways.

We will be doing this practice a lot on our journey—learning how to look through windows together—because these windows are one of my devices to build equity for us. I hope these stories speak to what is universal about every math teacher's professional landscape in a way that creates space for you to make your own meaning that is personally unique to you. By uncovering what we have in common, we create opportunities to elevate each other's voice and build a shared appreciation about *who we are as unique teachers*. Looking through these windows together is my way to enhance your professional identity so you can be more nourished by the work you do. And to position you as capable and empowered agents of your own professional learning *by inviting you to be windows for each other*. You and your colleagues, after all, are the most important windows on your journey.

This is why we steer clear of the blame game. It doesn't enhance us as professionals, nor does it foster our agency. We need to sidestep the unproductive debates that divide us so we can position ourselves to build a more *inclusive* and *empowering* culture of professionalism. That is how we will change the current narrative about how we grow and develop our teaching craft. The scaffolded activities explained at the end of this chapter will help us learn how to talk more productively about the unproductive results we are seeing in our classrooms.

Looking Through the Window: We All Crave a Sense of Professional Flourishment

Let's peer through this window together so we can identify one of the most essential truths about our professional landscape—given the insurmountable challenges we face, doing this job well requires a robust sense of something we will call "professional flourishment."

These teachers all have their own vision of equity they are trying to achieve with their teaching expertise.

Amanda, LeRon, and Alex have a vision for what student success looks like in their math classrooms. Amanda wants to see all her students have access and opportunities to engage in rigorous mathematics, regardless of where they are academically. Alex wants to see his students stand on their own two feet mathematically and build their intellectual resiliency as independent thinkers. LeRon wants to build an inclusive environment where he sees all of his students participating and showing him that they believe in themselves and they believe in him.

These teachers are nourished by human data that tells them they are achieving this vision of equity, and they're troubled by data that suggests their expertise is falling short of the outcomes they desire.

This human data nourishes each of them because it tells them that their teaching expertise is helping them author the math stories

Continued →

→ *Continued*

they want them to have. This data enhances their identity because it validates their sense of professional purpose and the reasons why they, presumably, wanted to become teachers in the first place.

That's why they're troubled by some of the student outcomes they are witnessing in their classroom—they recognize that their current level of expertise is falling short of achieving the vision of equity they desire. For Amanda, it's the sense that some students are falling behind, while others aren't being challenged. Alex sees students who won't take ownership over their learning. For LeRon, it's the data that tells him his students are quitting on themselves—and on him.

These teachers are looking for ways to flourish despite the seemingly insurmountable challenges they face.

They know that failure is an inherent part of teaching because *teaching is never perfect*. There is simply too much for them to overcome that is beyond the influence of their love, care, and instructional practice. But they want to do more than *just survive* day to day in their existing state. They desire a state where they can *continually thrive* year to year at achieving better outcomes for their students.

In our own unique ways, these teaching stories hold the same truths for us. We all have a vision of equity we are trying to achieve with our teaching expertise—a vision of a math class that enriches the lives of all our students and empowers them with a productive math story. When we witness growth in those we teach, our fulfillment from our work is not just professional, it's deeply personal. It feels good when we see them have positive and enjoyable experiences in our classroom. It *nourishes* our sense of efficacy and self-worth and validates our professional identity.

That's why it troubles us so much when we see students not experiencing success in our math classes. Because our professional struggles are very personal to us, we must have a sense of growing, of progressing, of getting better because we crave, like all people, a belief that we can *flourish* at what we love to do despite all the challenges in our way. This is what makes our current culture of professional development so frustrating and demoralizing. Not only does it not offer us a coherent pathway for getting better, it actually works against our efforts to improve our expertise of the instructional practices that will help us achieve our vision of equity. More on these "Headwinds" in a moment.

Defining Professional Flourishment

For the purposes of our journey, the concepts of "flourishing" and "nourishment" are intertwined in a positively reinforcing, symbiotic relationship that we will call "flourishment." When we feel good about our work, we're more inclined to get better at it. When we get better at it, we continue to feel even better about our work. Because it's an elevated and empowered state of being that will serve us well, I want to highlight three essential points:

Flourishment
the nourishing satisfaction we feel when our professional identity is enhanced and our sense of agency is activated. It is a portmanteau of "flourishing" and "nourishment."

➤ Flourishment is the *nourishing satisfaction we feel when our professional identity is enhanced*. We feel it when our practice is aligned and integrated with our purpose—when our expertise creates the human data that validates the reasons we became a teacher in the first place. It's the desired state of professional being where we feel the most fulfilled by our work—when we see students in our classrooms generating the math stories we want them to have as a result of our expertise.

➤ When we are experiencing flourishment, we are *empowered by a positive professional mindset that activates our sense of agency*. We are more inclined to take risks and try new things because we want to get better at our craft—we want to professionally flourish. We feel enthusiastic about our work and excited for math class and the unexpected challenges we may face—because our students are enthusiastic and excited for the unexpected challenges of the math class we've created for them. Setbacks and shortfalls in our performance are not discouraging obstacles, but opportunities to learn and improve. In this way, flourishment is the emotional result of a sustained growth mindset.

The Headwinds That Erode Our Professional Flourishment

The Headwinds in Figure 2.1 erode and rob us of our sense of professional flourishment. They are the systemic beliefs and actions that are *unproductive* to improving our teaching expertise. Peering into these Headwinds, we see the Beacons that were introduced previously. The Beacons are the teacher-centered beliefs and actions that are *productive* to building our culture of professionalism, improving our teaching expertise, and changing our cultural math story.

2.1　The Headwinds and the Beacons

The Headwinds		The Beacons
Efforts to reform the teaching and learning in math classrooms continue to come from the "top-down."	→	Our efforts to transform must come from the "inside-out."
We're incentivized to value what the system measures and how it's measured.	→	Motivation is fostered most when we calibrate our measures to our values.
We operate in a system of silos.	→	We must continually seek vantage, particularly from the students' perspective.
Effective math teaching is reduced to a recipe anybody can follow (or it's deemed an innate gift only some of us have).	→	Effective math teaching is a craft we can study best through each other.

For decades, the current climate in education, with its "addiction to reform" and its obsession with improving standardized test data, has created a system that isn't capable of meeting our professional needs—not because individuals in the system want it that way, but because the system serves its own needs, not ours. Our need—a robust sense of professional flourishment—is a uniquely individual need requiring a teacher-centered approach to improving the teaching and learning of mathematics in the classroom. We work in a top-down management system designed to do different things like standardize the teaching and learning of mathematics, establish tools of accountability and assessment, and enforce compliance to mandates by attaching funding to performance, and to do these tasks as efficiently as possible in a one-size-fits-all bureaucratic approach.

FURTHER LEARNING

For a richer context of the issue and a deeper understanding of some of the language I am using in this book, check out John Merrow's interview with Drew Perkins on Episode 53 of the *Teach Thought* podcast.

To understand the needs of the system, I offer you this data point. In 2015, *The Every Student Succeeds Act,* the federal legislation that funds public education, passed Congress with strong bipartisan support and was signed into law by President Obama. In that legislation, the words "accountability" and "assessment" appear 265 and 250 times, respectively. Want to take a guess at how many times the words "learning" and "teaching" appear in the legislation?

Twelve and eight, respectively.

I promise I'm not cherry-picking data here. The continued focus on assessment data continually threatens our sense of nourishment—our sense that our work adds value to the lives of our students. Most of us didn't become teachers because we're deeply passionate about training students how to get right answers on standardized tests. It's not a part of our vision of equity. Our teaching souls are nourished by more noble calls to action such as social justice, equity and fairness, and the emotional well-being and intellectual development of the young people we teach.

> Examinations of achievement scores alone can never reveal how the scores might be improved.
>
> —Stigler and Hiebert, *The Teaching Gap* (1999, p. 7)

The practice of using standardized test data as the major metric of progress and growth also hinders our ability to flourish because it does not offer us a direction for getting better as teachers. The goal of raising test scores has left math teachers with no coherent pathway—no *focus*—for professional growth. The math scores of our students, after all, will never tell us *how* to improve our teaching for our students because it doesn't tell us what our students need. Why did they get the answer wrong? *We never know.*

> It is surprising and somewhat discouraging how little attention has been paid to the intimate nature of teaching and school learning in the debates on education that have raged over the past decade. These debates have been so focused on performance and standards that they have mostly overlooked the means by which teachers and pupils alike go about their business in real-life classrooms—how teachers teach and how pupils learn.
>
> —Bruner, *The Culture of Education* (1996, p. 86)

As mentioned previously, perhaps the strongest Headwind working against our professional growth as math teachers is the fact that we work in a system that, for decades, has normalized a culture of professional isolationism. The siloing effect of school structures and our teaching schedules

▸ prevent us from developing the collegial relationships we need so we can become more active partners in each other's professional growth,

- deny us opportunities to develop a shared understanding about each other's visions of equity and a shared appreciation for how each of us are going about accomplishing it, and

- block avenues for seeking the vantage we need to identify and move away from unproductive actions we are currently taking in our classroom.

Striving for Equity Requires a Little Bit of Sisu

Sisu
the quality of sustaining hardened grit and tireless resolve in the face of persistent and insurmountable obstacles.

The Headwinds are not your fault. They are simply persistent, systemic forces and unproductive beliefs that erode our individual flourishment. Like a sailor learning how to tack a boat back and forth to make headway against the wind, we must learn how to navigate the Headwinds to make gains on our journey together—because there will always be tensions between the needs of the system and our needs as individuals who work within that system.

There's a wonderful Finnish word *sisu*—and it's useful for our conversation on flourishment. Representing one of the core values of Finnish culture, there is no literal translation for sisu in English. I understand sisu to be the personal quality of sustaining hardened grit and tireless resolve in the face of persistent and insurmountable obstacles. As we saw in the three windows above, I think it's a quality that every passionate math teacher needs to possess in order to remain resilient. I don't use sisu as a negative word with grim connotations. It is about finding flourishment in the reward of doing labor that may never achieve success. Let me offer two quick anecdotes to help bring some more context to sisu and how it relates to flourishment.

The Starfish Story

An old man approaches a boy throwing starfish back into the ocean.

Old Man: *What are you doing?*

Boy: *I'm saving these starfish by throwing them back.*

Old Man: *Don't you see that there's too many to save? You can't make a difference.*

Boy, looking down at the starfish in his hand before throwing it back: *It makes a difference to this one.*

By focusing on the data that motivates him despite the obvious insurmountable obstacles, this boy is exercising sisu. It doesn't matter that he can't save them all. There's still important work to be done.

The "77-7" Story

Back in the days when I coached high school basketball, we once lost a game 77-7. Needless to say, we weren't very competitive that season, and we were woefully outmatched in most games. This game was particularly brutal because *all seven of our points came in the first quarter.* That means, for the last three quarters of a basketball game, we went scoreless. Over that time, every possession ended in a missed shot or—far more frequently—a turnover. We didn't even convert a single free throw—and we had six.

At some point near the beginning of the fourth quarter, we were down by 50 points and the "running clock" mercy rule went into effect, drastically shortening actual playing time. When my players found this out, they were pissed. They didn't want mercy—they wanted as much playing time as they could get regardless of the outcome. Losing by more than 50 points and seeing my players use our time-outs to keep as much playing time on the clock as possible, was one of my most memorable moments as a coach. It was an expression of sisu that still moves me to smile to this day.

I bring up sisu because equity is an ideal we are *striving for.* Creating math classrooms where our instructional craft positions every student in ways that enhance their identity and foster their agency is something we can *approach,* but rarely, if ever, achieve. Some days we'll be overwhelmed by the scope of our challenges. We can't throw all the starfish back in a day. And some of our starfish, even after we throw them, still land short of the water's edge. But every math lesson, like every possession in a basketball game, is a chance to do something better than you did before.

Sisu is about embracing our nature as being imperfect and unfinished. It is at the core of flourishment and the first Beacon.

Flourishment, the First Beacon, and Staying Unfinished

> Let's get one thing out of the way right up front. It may seem natural to assume that [experts] have some rare gift of willpower or "grit" or "stick-to-itiveness" that the rest of us just lack, but that would be a mistake for two reasons. First there is very little scientific evidence for the existence of a general "willpower" that can be applied to any situation. Once you assume that [these traits are] innate, it automatically becomes something you can't do anything about. This sort of circular thinking ... is worse than useless; it is damaging in that it can convince people that they might as well not even try.
>
> —Ericsson and Pool, *Peak: Secrets From the New Science of Expertise* (2017)

In addition to being concerned about Brenda and our cultural math story, I'm concerned about our collective sense of flourishment and the overall health and vitality of the math teaching profession. As our cultural enthusiasm for mathematics has waned, so too has professional enthusiasm for teaching mathematics. And it will continue to wane until we do something differently—like create a culture of professionalism that can help us find more flourishment in our work.

I recognize that challenging these Headwinds and embracing these Beacons requires energy and courage because they ask us to upset the homeostasis in ourselves. They invite more unpredictability into our already disjointed and chaotic professional landscape. Transformation always does. I'm not going to sugarcoat it—improving your craft is going to be uncomfortable work at times. And a greater sense of flourishment is the only reward I can offer you. I know it may sound silly, but the only reward for doing the uncomfortable work it takes to see more of your students experience success in math class is seeing more of your students experiencing success in math class. And the only one who cares about that reward is us—not the system we work in.

That's what the first Beacon is all about. Your desire to transform must come from the inside-out. You already know this.

KEY TAKEAWAYS FROM CHAPTER 2

* Looking through windows to see what is universally true for all of us and uniquely true to each of us is a device to build equity into our journey. Along our journey, you will learn how to be windows for each other so that you can be more active partners in each other's professional learning.

* Flourishment is the nourishing satisfaction we feel when our professional identity is enhanced and our sense of agency is activated. It is the necessary mindset for our journey.

* While every teacher has a vision of equity they are trying to achieve through their teaching, full equity is an ideal. It is not something we are often able to achieve due to the insurmountable obstacles on our landscape. Yet, we persevere because we all crave professional flourishment. Sisu.

* The first Beacon tells us that the desire to change must come from within us. A greater sense of professional flourishment is something we can only bring about for ourselves and each other.

INTERLUDE 2:
THE STRUCTURED ACTIVITIES
ON OUR JOURNEY

In Interlude 2, you will be introduced to the three activities that will give our journey coherence and structure—Lighthouse Reflections, Seek Vantages, and Campfire Gatherings. Beginning in Part 2, future interludes will contain these activities with specific prompts to reflect, calibrate, and collaborate on ways to expand your teaching potential and improve your expertise.

LIGHTHOUSE REFLECTIONS

FOCUS

What are they?

Lighthouse Reflections are prompts designed to help you *practice focusing* on the things you value most as a teacher of mathematics and identify the data—the measures—that will motivate you to further your teaching expertise.

How do they work?

Taking anywhere between 10 and 20 minutes to complete, these reflections are moments to engage in purposeful deep thought about your own beliefs and your actions in the classroom. The depth of our learning is a function of the depth of authenticity and attention that we put into these reflections. When you spend time focusing on who you are and what you believe, you are becoming a more valuable window for your colleagues.

Why a "lighthouse"?

A "Lighthouse Reflection" serves the same function that a lighthouse does for sailors—a guiding light to help them keep their bearings and monitor their progress. ✊

SEEK VANTAGE

VANTAGE

What are they?

A Seek Vantage is a guided observation that will help you *practice gaining new vantage* on the teaching and learning of mathematics in your own classroom. Seeing someone teach inherently encourages us to see our own teaching differently. Seeing the learning needs of someone else's students invites us to think more deeply about the learning needs of our own students. These observations are the moments we purposefully seek data that will help us refine and improve our own mental model of what we are seeing in our own classrooms.

How do they work?

When time in your schedule permits, complete these guided observations. Remember, there is no pacing plan to our journey. There is no suggested minimum amount of time to spend observing in each other's classrooms. Is 15 minutes a week enough? An hour? Three lessons a month? You will need to decide what is enough for you given your professional schedules. But I ask that you make a commitment to continue the practice of seeking vantage as regularly as you can in as many different classrooms as feasible. I promise you. It's worth it.

Why a "boat"?

The Boat reminds us that we must leave the silos of our classrooms if we are to embark on this "voyage of discovery," to bring us back to Proust's imagery about learning to see our landscape with new eyes. ⚓

CAMPFIRE GATHERING

RELATIONSHIPS

What are they?

Expert performers *build relationships* with colleagues because they know they will need help seeing what they cannot see for themselves. We must do the same. Campfire Gatherings are guided conversations that will help build the type of trusting relationships you will need on this journey—relationships that will position you as active partners in each other's professional growth. Campfire Gatherings help us practice the conversation skills we need to *enhance each other's identity and foster their sense of agency* as we learn to talk productively about the unproductive outcomes in our classrooms.

How do they work?

For each Campfire Gathering, you will have an agenda to follow. Having a trusted and caring coach facilitate these Campfire Gatherings could be helpful, but I've written these agendas in a way that empowers you to conduct them on your own with each other. The questions, prompts, and activities are carefully crafted to set you up for success as you learn to conduct these meetings for yourself. Designed for groups of three to four teachers, these conversations take about an hour to complete and should happen at an uninterrupted moment of your day, most commonly after school. Pairs will most likely have shorter conversations. Groups larger than four may require longer gatherings.

Why a "campfire?"

For countless generations, the campfire has been a setting for humans to engage in storytelling and acts of self-expression, to build trust and share wisdom, and to foster relationships and culture—a shared understanding of who "we" are, collectively and individually. Because a campfire is one of the most ancient and universal settings for humans to engage in the type of relationship building that we want to focus on, it is our symbol for these gatherings. ●

> online resources ↘ **Further Your Craft:** You can download and follow the Campfire Group Facilitation Guide from bit.ly/3o7bBzq, visit the *The Imperfect and Unfinished Math Teacher* Free Resources tab on the Corwin website.

Planning Ahead

Beginning in Chapter 4, you will be invited to participate in your first Seek Vantage and Campfire Gathering. To plan for upcoming Seek Vantage activities, you will need to schedule time in your schedule to observe the teaching and learning of mathematics. If you're still facing obstacles for finding that time, see Interlude 1 for scheduling strategies. To plan for the upcoming Campfire Gatherings, you will need to schedule time in your schedule to meet collectively. Most teachers do this after school.

If you haven't already, connect with your colleagues to schedule these activities.

NOTES

3

EXPANDING OUR POTENTIAL WITH DELIBERATE PRACTICE

Where We've Been

In Chapter 1, you were invited to embark on a journey to see our professional landscape with new eyes so that we can become more active partners in each other's professional growth. In Chapter 2, we explored the idea of flourishment—the necessary mindset for our journey.

Where We're Going

In Chapter 3, we will explore "deliberate practice" and the necessary actions for sustaining our sense of flourishment. We will also go deeper into the language we will use on our journey to further our teaching expertise.

We are not born with fixed abilities, and those who achieve at the highest level do not do so because of their genetics. The myth that our brains are fixed and that we simply don't have the aptitude for certain topics is not only scientifically inaccurate; it is omnipresent and negatively impacts education and many other events in our everyday lives.

—Jo Boaler, *Limitless Mind: Learn, Lead, and Live Without Barriers* (2019)

How Did Timur Get That Good?

A Story About Timur

How good is chess grandmaster Timur Gareyev?

On December 3 and 4, 2016, at the age of 29, he played 48 games of chess against 48 different players. Out of those 48 games, he won 35, had seven draws, and lost six.

That's pretty good, right? Wait, there's more.

He played all of these games simultaneously—taking on each opponent at once. All 48 games started at the same time and the longest one lasted about 19 hours.

That's really good, right? Wait for it . . .

He played these games *blindfolded*. Yeah. Let that sink in for just a moment. Timur never saw a chessboard and never touched a chess piece for any of these games. A messenger verbally relayed moves back and forth between Timur and his opponents—opponents, remember, who were only playing a single game (against Timur) in front of a chessboard they could see, but Timur had to remember (along with 47 other chessboards).

That's ridiculously good, right? I mean, how did he get *that good*?

Our Current Potential Is Always an Expandable Vessel

" . . . there's no such thing as a predefined ability. The brain is adaptable, and training can create skills . . . that did not exist before . . . Potential is an expandable vessel. We can create our own potential.

—Ericsson and Pool, *Peak: Secrets From the New Science of Expertise* (2017)

> **Random fun fact**
> Timur rode the equivalent of 50 miles on a stationary bike while playing these games. Maybe we have something to learn from him about letting our students physically move so they can focus on learning mathematics?

Anders Ericsson has been asking this question of experts for several decades now: *How did they get that good?* His research on the methods of practice and habits of mind of expert performers—people like Timur who exhibit a high degree of craftsmanship at performing complex skills—shows us that human potential is an expandable vessel. Anyone, at any level, can continue to improve their expertise by learning to do things that they could not previously do. And the most effective way to expand our potential is to engage in "deliberate practice"—the gold standard when it comes to the *type of practice* that optimizes improvements in performance. Deliberate practice is not simply about finding ways to improve your expertise—it's about finding ways to *improve how you improve* so you can increase the *efficiency of your efficacy.*

Looking Through the Window: The Core Elements of Deliberate Practice

Deliberate practice remains the gold standard for anyone in any field who wishes to take advantage of the gift of adaptability in order to build new skills and abilities . . . Even if your field is one in which deliberate practice in the strictest sense is not possible, you can still use the principles of deliberate practice as a guide to developing the most effective sort of practice possible in your area.

—Ericsson and Pool, *Peak: Secrets From the New Science of Expertise* (2017)

Before we look through this window together, let me state the obvious: the challenges of becoming a better math teacher are quite different from the challenges of becoming a better chess player. Timur doesn't have to worry about his chess pieces bullying each other, or not getting enough sleep, or being absent. He doesn't need to build a culture of inclusion and share authority with his pieces before they buy-in to his decisions. The skills we need to do our job well are always changing because our students aren't pawns—they have evolving math identities that affect their agency. Students have imaginations and the ability to form stories about who they are and what math class is about—beliefs that inform how they behave in class. Chess pieces obviously do not.

Furthermore, a chess match is a closed, controlled system. There is always a best move that is more advantageous over all the others, and oftentimes there are several good moves. Timur can study objective data immediately after each game to see the exact moment(s) where he made inaccuracies, mistakes, or blunders and see clearly what he could've done better. His options for reflection are plentiful and the data he has is extremely accurate and forever useful.

By comparison, teaching is influenced by countless variables that we must continually navigate with in-the-moment decisions. In our lessons, we face dilemmas with no clear "best" moves—situations where what seems like a good move from some students seems like it might be a mistake, or even a blunder, for others. And we rarely get to analyze the data of our lesson—and never in the ways Timur can—because so much of our data is subjective and filtered through the lens of our lived experiences. After our math lessons, we're collecting exit tickets that some students didn't have enough time to complete, resetting our classroom spaces, and wondering if we have time to go to the bathroom before next period.

While our challenges to improving our expertise are quite different from Timur's, the actions are the same for us as they are for anyone who wants to *increase the efficiency of their efficacy* at improving any skill—we must engage in the Core Elements of Deliberate Practice. Let's look through the window of Timur's expertise to understand the Core Elements in a context outside of our profession before exploring how it supports our goal of becoming better math teachers.

Expanding his potential as a chess player has always been dependent on his ability to sustain his own sense of *flourishment*.

The game of chess continues to offer Timur the flourishment he needs to keep furthering his level of performance. Despite discouraging frustrations and long plateaus with minimal gains in improvement, he has never been satisfied with his current level of performance for very long. He regularly upsets the homeostasis in himself so he could achieve things he had not been able to do before. At every step of the way, through tens of thousands of hours of practice, becoming a better chess player continues to be an endeavor that nourishes him in ways that make it worth the investment of time, energy, and emotions it takes to keep flourishing.

In a sense, Timur became incredibly good at chess because chess offered him the flourishment he needed to remain an unfinished chess player through tens of thousands of hours of playing chess imperfectly. Timur has been able to *sustain* that level of flourishment by consistently investing his time and energy doing the next three things.

Continued →

→ *Continued*

1: Timur strategically *focuses* on attainable goals he values and on data that continually motivates him to keep expanding his potential.

Ever since Timur started learning the rules and basic principles of chess, he has focused on the attainable performance goals that mattered to him enough that he wanted to go through the work of purposefully practicing and refining the actions that would help him attain those goals. If the rewards of getting better weren't worth it, he wouldn't have continued to get better—he would have been finished long ago. To sustain his flourishment, he continually monitors and measures his progress by focusing on data that nourishes him and fills him with a rewarding sense of accomplishment. He also willingly seeks out and focuses on data that exposes his weaknesses in ways that empower him to follow a productive plan of action moving forward.

Timur sustains his sense of flourishment by regularly asking these focusing questions: What does getting better look like next? What specific actions will help me get better? How can I refine my practice of these actions?

2: Timur actively shifts his *vantage*, learning how to see the game of chess—and his own thinking—with new eyes.

Much like changing a workout routine can increase an athlete's level of fitness, creating novel challenges helps Timur develop a healthy habit of disrupting his routine in ways that help him identify unproductive beliefs. One way Timur did this was to spend time watching and studying others play countless games of chess. Freed from the demands of having to make decisions, he could watch how the consequences of moves play out without concern or judgment, seeing structure in the game and the relationships of the pieces in ways that he might not have seen before. He could see missed opportunities he might not have otherwise noticed, and he could wonder about the missed opportunities he doesn't yet see in his own practice.

Timur shifts his vantage not just so he can refine his knowledge of the game of chess, but so he can *refine his identity as a learner of the craft*. To improve, Timur needed to shift his vantage on his current mental model by seeking data that helped him evaluate the effectiveness of his own practice on a metacognitive level. He needed to *actively seek* out unproductive loops of confirmation bias—examples of beliefs and actions that weren't working for him but are still *tacit* to him. Sometimes this meant he had to admit that he was wrong about his beliefs or his practice so he could focus on a new approach and take steps backward in the short term so he could further his craft in the long term.

In this space of vantage, Timur can more productively ask himself: What blind spots might I have that are unproductive to improving my skills? What actions am I taking that might be unproductive to achieving my performance goals? *What beliefs might I be wrong about?*

3: Timur continually fosters *relationships* that position himself and others in ways that further their craft individually, collectively, and culturally.

Timur's achievements are a result of the efforts of others *to help him see what he could not see for himself.* He has sustained his flourishment because others helped him sustain it when he could not go it alone. These relationships help Timur and others develop a rich and robust sense of appreciation for each other's ability to further each other's learning. In this culture of professionalism, they challenge and push each other because they recognize that their individual sense of flourishment is intimately tied to their collective sense of flourishment. If one of them improves, they all improve. In this way, relationships help build a collective sense of efficacy for himself and his colleagues.

In these relationships, Timur and his colleagues regularly ask each other: What do you see? And how do you see it?

Timur is doing the things anybody needs to do if they want to keep expanding their potential and increase their performance of a complex craft. His craft gives him the *flourishment* he needs to remain unfinished. And he seeks to sustain his sense of flourishment by engaging in *focus*, seeking *vantage*, and building *relationships*—all in an effort to find ways to improve his mental model and understanding of the game.

Expanding our potential as math teachers is dependent on sustaining our internal sense of flourishment. We can sustain our sense of flourishment best when we engage in the following Core Elements of Deliberate Practice (Figure 3.1):

RELATIONSHIPS

DELIBERATE PRACTICE

FOCUS

VANTAGE

▶ Strategically *focus* on attainable goals we value and continually seek data that fosters our sense of agency and motivates us to keep expanding our potential.

- Actively shift our *vantage* on our professional practice and learn to see our professional landscape with new eyes.

- Continually foster *relationships* that position ourselves in ways that further our craft individually, collectively, and culturally.

3.1. Aligning the Core Elements with the Beacons and the activities

The first Beacon reminds us that our efforts to transform must come from the inside-out. Flourishment is something we must learn to create for ourselves by learning how to expand our potential. Our sense of flourishment can best be sustained when we engage in the following Core Elements of Deliberate Practice.

Core Element	Sustaining flourishment requires us to . . .	Structured Activity	Aligning Beacon
FOCUS	Strategically focus on attainable goals we value and on data that motivates us to keep expanding our potential.	Lighthouse Reflection	Motivation is fostered most when we calibrate our measures to our values.
VANTAGE	Actively shift our vantage on our professional practice and learn to see our professional landscape with new eyes.	Seek Vantage	We must continue to seek vantage by looking through windows, particularly from the student perspective.
RELATIONSHIPS	Continually foster relationships that position ourselves in ways that further our craft individually, collectively, and culturally.	Campfire Gathering	Effective math teaching is a craft we can study best through each other.

Although I present focus, vantage, and relationships in that order, they are not steps in a sequence. And although I show them in a double-arrowed circle, deliberate practice is not a strictly cyclical process. They are *components* that are woven together as an integrated fabric.

And they are things we should be doing whenever we can, not just during the structured activities. You will see the lighthouse, boat, and campfire icons in other areas of this book when I invite you to think of focus, vantage, or relationships in more informal ways.

Lighthouse Reflection, Seek Vantage, or Campfire Gathering should be viewed as *a subset* of ways we can use focus, vantage, and relationships to grow our teaching craft. We should be focusing on what we value most as often as we can as we navigate our lessons. We should be seeking vantage as frequently as we can—making the most of our pupil-free time to look at teaching and learning in the math classroom from the students' perspective. Our relationship building and how we position ourselves as active partners in each other's professional growth is not limited to Campfire Gatherings. They are just structured opportunities for you to deliberately practice the communication skills you need to be practicing in regular conversations with each other. We should always be using language in ways that enhance each other's identity and foster their sense of agency—*because that's what equity is all about.*

What We Believe Affects What We See

We all see something different,
all recall something different
when we watch the parade go marching through.
So be kind to all of your neighbors
'cause they're just like you.
And you're nothing special unless they are too.

—Typhoon, "The Honest Truth" (2011)

In Chapter 4, we are going to look into Lillian's classroom together. Before we do, we first need to establish some language so we can discuss what we see. You already have a very complex, preexisting mental model of your professional landscape and your role as a teacher of mathematics. And you already have some existing understanding about some of the unproductive results you are seeing in your classroom—the math stories that you would like to change with your expertise. As a result, you probably have some strong beliefs about what you will see in each other's classrooms and some of the decisions you're making. What these beliefs are—how you interpret what you see—is shaped by the mental models you have about math teaching and your professional identity:

- As caring colleagues invested in each other's sense of flourishment, how do we talk about our beliefs in ways that enhance each other's identity and foster each other's sense of agency?

- As caring stewards invested in the math stories of all our students, how do we talk about the impact of our actions in the classroom without feeling shame about our expertise?

- How do we create a safe, nurturing environment that will help us be authentic windows for each other and empower us to talk productively about the unproductive results in our classroom?

Language and the Core Elements of Deliberate Practice

Because our ways of thinking about our professional landscape are limited by the language we have to describe it, our new culture of professionalism will require us to develop our own language—our own way of describing our professional landscapes to each other.

You may be asking, *Is all this language necessary?* Yes. Creating language is an essential component of deliberate practice and rooted in Ericsson's research. Timur and other experts use their own language because it helps them think about their craft in ways that create new opportunities to expand their potential, to find new avenues for growth. Language also helps experts "chunk" complex ideas and helps them engage in a form of data compression, freeing up space for more thinking, and uncover ways we can increase the efficiency of efficacy, for ourselves and for each other.

> Much of deliberate practice involves developing ever more efficient mental representations that you can use in whatever activity you are practicing . . . This is a major advantage of highly developed mental representations: you can assimilate and consider a great deal more information at once.
>
> —Ericsson and Pool, *Peak: Secrets From the New Science of Expertise* (2017)

Generating language for ourselves will be an important strategy on our journey for three specific reasons, each aligning with one of the Core Elements of Deliberate Practice:

- New language helps us identify preexisting understandings that were previously tacit—allowing us to bring them into *focus*.

- Language helps us create an internal sense of *vantage* that increases our ability to see our own professional landscape with new eyes.

- Language helps us build *relationships* that can position each other as active partners in each other's growth. It's how we further the craft of teaching not just individually, but collectively and culturally.

The Island of Practice

Like the Beacons and looking through windows, the language in the Island of Practice (Figure 3.2) is a device to build equity into our journey, keeping our journey cohesive to all and inclusive for each in ways that enhance our identity and foster our collective sense of agency. The language I'm offering is only a starting point for you and your colleagues. You will further this language organically in ways that you need. That's what experts do!

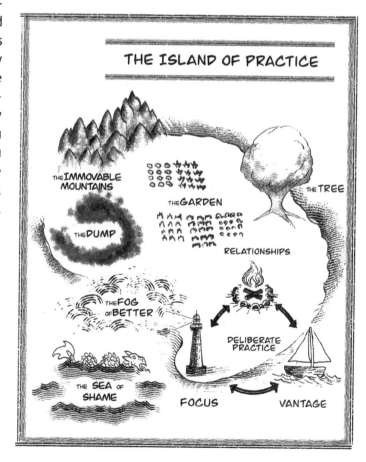

3.2. The Island of Practice

Much of this language chunks ideas that we've talked about before. For example,

> We see the images that represent the *Core Elements of Deliberate Practice*—the actions we need to take to sustain our sense of flourishment.

> We discussed the Headwinds and other external forces that continually erode your flourishment—such as standardized tests, grading, class size, content standards, bell schedules. These *Immovable Mountains* are things we cannot change through improvements in our teaching alone.

> We're passionate about what we do, and we care deeply about the quality of our work. We have moments when we're not feeling very nourished by what we see in our math classes. The *Sea of Shame* is there to remind us that we all need a sense of nourishment from our work and why it's important to build relationships that give each other the grace we need in order to do this work productively.

> When we want to get better at meeting student needs, but don't know what to do or what to do differently, we feel lost in *The Fog of Better*—a space where we don't know how to flourish against the discouraging data we're seeing. The Fog of Better is there to remind ourselves that in order to flourish, we must focus on data that helps us monitor our progress and motivates us to improve.

Next we get to the major features that we will be discussing at length in this book: the Garden, the Dump, and the Tree. Because flourishment is found when we improve and become more productive in our understanding about our beliefs and actions, these are the features on our Island of Practice we must constantly learn to see with new eyes:

> *The Garden:* The Garden represents the system of learning you create through your actions in the classroom. It represents your teaching *how*. From your perspective, your Garden is where you exercise your professional agency. From your students' perspectives, the Garden is where they author their math story. It's what they call "math class."

> *The Dump:* At the edge of your Garden sits the Dump. It is the place where your teaching *how* falls short of achieving your vision of equity. It represents the human data that suggests your students are not authoring the math stories you want them to have— it is data you want to change.

> *The Tree:* . . .

I Call It a Tree; You May See It Differently

In the Introduction, when you put yourself in my shoes with Rudy, a voice inside you told you what you should do. What do you call that voice? Your mojo, chi, fire, moral compass, creed? What image would you use to represent your teaching *why?* I see mine as a Tree, much like the imagery associated with the "tree of life." Some teachers, like Parker Palmer, call it the "teaching soul." This may be an apt way for you to think about what I mean by the "Tree." But I also want to be inclusive of teachers who are on this journey but may not identify with this religious imagery.

LANGUAGE NOTE

I will continue to use the word "grace" throughout this book, and I recognize it has some religious overtones. I find it an extremely inclusive and useful word to describe our ways of relating to each other and our students.

Throughout our journey, I try to use language and imagery that are universal to all people and all cultures. I have also tried to choose language that reveals some truth about the nature of the thing it describes. The Island reminds us that we work in silos. Mountains are often looming obstacles in our way. It's hard to see and find direction in a Fog. The Garden is something you nurture and grow, but which you can easily replant and start anew each year—much like our classrooms. The Dump is simply a way to destigmatize our failures—we're all imperfect. The lighthouse, boat, and campfire are all images that represent what they do—focus, vantage, and relationships, respectively.

For me, a Tree is a useful image because it is a majestic, elaborate, and sacred system of life and vitality. It is a noble thing worthy of reverence. Just like you. It also needs nourishment and care over time. And it flourishes and thrives *when it is pruned*. All of these are useful ways to think about our teaching "self" on our journey. So, if I may, I'd like to continue to use the Tree as an image to think about our professional identity. It is something sacred that you are always carrying with you—a growing, living thing that craves nourishment.

KEY TAKEAWAYS FROM CHAPTER 3

* Our teaching potential is an expandable vessel, and we can further our potential most efficiently by engaging in the Core Elements of Deliberate Practice—focus, vantage, and relationships. Together, these actions sustain our sense of professional flourishment.

* What we see is heavily influenced by what we already believe. Creating new language can help us create new vantage on our existing beliefs and actions—especially the unproductive ones that are still currently tacit to us.

* The Island of Practice offers us language to describe a professional landscape that is universally true for all of us and uniquely true to each of us. The purpose of this language is to help us create new vantage on our deeply held beliefs about who we are as teachers and what we see in our classrooms.

INTERLUDE 3:
YOUR VISION OF EQUITY

You already have a vision of equity that you are trying to create through your teaching expertise. What yours looks like—and how you go about achieving it—is unique to you. We will go deeper and develop a more rigorous understanding of what the research says about how equitable teaching practices should look, sound, and feel like in the math classroom as we go along. For now, we'll start this journey with the most important vision of equity—your current one.

There are no right or wrong answers here—only imperfect and unfinished ones. You will be building on and elaborating these answers throughout our journey together.

YOUR VISION OF EQUITY

FOCUS

Imagine we bump into each other at a conference and have this exchange:

> Me: *How's math class going for your students?*
>
> You: *You know, I'm really enjoying teaching math right now and my students are enjoying class too!*
>
> Me: *Sweet! It sounds like you're feeling a lot of flourishment. Tell me more.*

Whatever you say next reveals a lot about what you're trying to achieve in the classroom (your vision of equity) and how you measure your own success as a teacher (your sense of flourishment).

- What is your vision of equity that you are trying to achieve through your teaching?

- What type of math stories do you want your students to author?

  - When students walk out of your classroom at the end of the school year, what do you want them to say about themselves as mathematical thinkers?

  - How do you want them to act when they face mathematical challenges in their lives, either in future academic classes or in real-world situations?

Continued →

→ *Continued*

● What data are you seeing in your classroom that encourages you and feeds your sense of flourishment? What data are you seeing that discourages you and deprives you of flourishment?
Now look at your current teaching practice with "new eyes."

● What new thinking and wondering has the word "flourishment" revealed about your identity and sense of agency as a teacher of mathematics? ●

PART 2

BUILDING OUR NEW CULTURE OF PROFESSIONALISM

4

CREATING VANTAGE TO TEST BELIEFS

Where We've Been

In Part 1, you were invited on a journey to see your professional landscape with new eyes. The Beacons will be our guiding principles as we learn how to create our culture of professionalism and become active partners in each other's professional growth. The Core Elements of Deliberate Practice will be the actions that will help us build this culture moving forward.

Where We're Going

In Part 2, we will take actions to build our new culture of professionalism. In Chapter 4, we will look into Lillian's sixth grade classroom and the dilemmas she's facing. We'll talk about why she's stuck—and what she can do to get herself unstuck.

Our mental models determine what we see. In any new experience, most people are drawn to take in and remember only the information that reinforces their existing mental models . . . . Because mental models are usually tacit, existing below the level of awareness, they are often untested and unexamined. They are generally invisible to us—until we look for them.

—Senge, Schools That Learn (2014, pp. 99-100)

A Window: Lillian's Classroom

We're about to walk into Lillian's sixth grade classroom. It's the end of the sixth week of school, and she's struggling with a common problem of practice many of us face: teaching grade-level content to students who demonstrate below-grade-level understanding. This can create particularly pressing dilemmas at the beginning of the school year as we try to get to know our students and determine what they understand (and what they don't) in an effort to identify and meet their learning needs—all while feeling the time crunch to begin teaching our grade-level content.

As we watch Lillian's lesson and listen to her reflections, let's give her some grace, regard her like we would one of our own beloved colleagues, and remember that she, like us, is on her own journey to finding her flourishment.

FOCUS QUESTIONS

FOCUS

As you read, I invite you to think about the following questions:

What is Lillian's vision of equity? What is she trying to achieve through her teaching expertise?

What is the data that Lillian sees that is troubling her? And more important, *why* does this data bother her so much? ●

Lillian's Classroom

Lillian is about 10 minutes into her lesson when we walk through the door. From our vantage in the room, we see her students sitting in groups of four and taking notes. We sense the academic energy—all students seem to be on point and focused on the task at hand. We see her at the board explaining the formal long division algorithm involving decimals in the divisor and dividend. We see the "Dad Mom Sister Brother" mnemonic device written on the board to prompt students through the divide, multiply, subtract, and "bring down" sequence of steps. After finishing up her direct instruction, she tells her students to begin working on the long division problems on their worksheets. *Let's get ready for the test tomorrow!*

Continued →

→ *Continued*

Lillian heads directly to a group of students, as if by habit, and provides some further guidance. We wonder if this is perhaps the group that struggles the most. After 3 minutes, she begins to walk around the room. She doesn't get far before a student asks a question. She stops for 30 seconds to answer. Again, she doesn't get far before another student asks her a question. Then another. She pauses to look around the room. A few groups are busy crunching away. They appear to have already mastered the skill. But many haven't moved past the first problem.

She makes a noticeable sigh. Perhaps it's frustration, maybe even exasperation. She stops the class and walks to the board. *Let me show you one more time how to do these. It's not hard if you just follow the steps, OK?* We walk out of the room as she begins to model another problem for her students.

After class, Lillian shares her thoughts on how the lesson went. She's clearly frustrated and venting emotion as she's telling her story. Her sense of flourishment is low to say the least.

My students aren't ready for sixth grade math. They don't know the basics! Every year, they come in with so many holes I have to fill. Their test scores from fifth grade show it. And most did poorly on the beginning-of-the-year diagnostic assessment that the district gave us. How are they going to learn proportions if they don't know equivalent fractions? And if they can't do decimals, then they can't do percentages and some of the geometry stuff. I don't have time to teach it conceptually so I just end up resorting to the algorithm because I need them all to be ready to move on.

But this group is moving so slowly. Some still aren't getting it. I was hoping to test them on it tomorrow, but after today's lesson, I don't think they're all ready to show mastery. But if today's lesson didn't work, will it work any better tomorrow? I don't know what else to do to get them ready for what they need to learn next.

Looking Through the Window: Lillian's Stuck but She Doesn't See It—Yet

In Chapter 3, we learned that one of the ways Timur improves his craft is by shifting his vantage and *actively seeking out* his own unproductive loops of confirmation bias—examples of existing beliefs and current courses of actions that aren't productive for him but are still, at the moment, *tacit* to him. Sometimes this means admitting he needs to change something in his own actions or beliefs in order to free up space in his practice—and his brain—to focus on new, potentially more productive approaches. Creating vantage is a habit any professional can practice to help them see what they need to see to get themselves unstuck. And vantage is what Lillian needs right now because she's stuck in one of these unproductive loops of confirmation bias.

Lillian has a strong belief in making sure her students are ready for the mathematics they need to learn next. It's a noble belief. Every caring math teacher should be motivated to get their students ready for whatever math challenges they may face in the world—academic or otherwise. It's deeply rooted into each of our own visions of equity in some way because our Trees are nourished when our students show us data that tells us they are ready.

However, "ready" lacks the focus Lillian needs to get better at achieving "readiness." Ready is vague—*What does it look like?* It's not measurable—*What does ready mean?* It's not attainable—*Ready for what? Next year's math class? This year's standardized test? College? Career? Life skills?* In the absence of this clarity, Lillian does what every human does when they face a vague situation. She resorts to her instincts and the preexisting beliefs and actions—her mental models—that seem to have worked before. It's what the human brain is always doing—filling gaps with our intuition and jumping to conclusions before we have all the information we need. It's an essential coping skill our brains have created so it can make sense out of all the data we must perceive, process, analyze, and synthesize throughout our day.

Oftentimes, this means we take action without first *testing* and *interrogating* the *whys* behind our actions by stopping and asking ourselves: *What's really going on here? What might I not know yet about this situation? Am I seeing all the data? Am I interpreting the data I see accurately? Whose perspective might I be overlooking? What might I be wrong about?* These are the valuable questions of a "not knowing" mindset we talked about in the Introduction.

The important point here is this: you cannot test a belief you don't yet see. When we take action without constantly testing our own beliefs and questioning our actions, we risk getting stuck doing unproductive things in our Gardens like Lillian is doing now.

> The important point here is this: you cannot test a belief you don't yet see.

Lillian is already attached to her existing model—her vision—about what "ready" looks like. For her, ready would be all or almost all of her students showing mastery on fifth grade standardized assessments or whatever diagnostic test the district used. According to this measure, her current students don't meet her definition of "ready." And so she takes actions to create the data that she wants to see in her Garden—data that she believes shows the "readiness" she needs to achieve in her vision of equity. She creates a system of direct instruction with a heavy focus on showing mastery of the formal algorithms. To monitor her progress, she collects data she values—showing fluency on worksheet problems—but she keeps getting the same discouraging results. Her actions are reaffirming her beliefs—her students still aren't ready. Instead of changing course, she keeps at it, still not able to generate the data that will nourish her. And now she's flat out discouraged. Stuck.

There's nothing *wrong* about Lillian's vision of equity. But the tacit assumptions, conclusions, and beliefs she's created along the way are preventing her from moving further. They are simply unproductive. Like all of us, she's biased toward her own beliefs. We all want to believe that what we are doing is productive. That's why we constantly need to create vantage for ourselves so we can recognize moments when we're not productive, and learn to recognize them sooner.

SOME KEY QUESTIONS

FOCUS

What is something that you used to believe was true about effective math teaching, but no longer do?

What did it take to change your mind?

More important, *what would it have taken to change your mind sooner?* ❡

What's Next for Lillian?

So what's next for Lillian? How will she get the vantage she needs to see her current story with new eyes? If she were our colleague and we had a working relationship with Lillian, we could validate and mirror back her feelings: *You're frustrated because what you're doing isn't working for some of your students.* Then perhaps extend an invitation, such as *I've been doing a series of Math Talks to start my lessons as a way to fill these gaps for my students. It's not going perfectly, but I think it's helping. Want to start coming by and watching me do them? Maybe we can get better together.*

Odds are, we don't have that relationship *yet*. And even if we did, *sometimes we don't want to hear the advice of others*. If you've been someone's close friend or partner long enough, you know that you can't always just tell them what you think they need to hear. In all our relationships, we have to be mindful of the ears we are speaking to and what they are ready to hear. Even when we're asked for our vantage, we still must be careful. Our emotional selves—our Trees—can be stubborn things. When we are *willfully rooted* in what we believe and frustrated by our own inefficacy, our ears can become really small. And Lillian is kind of in that space. I don't want to have that conversation with her at this moment. *Do you?*

> When we are willfully rooted in what we believe and frustrated by our own inefficacy, our ears can become really small.

Perhaps the culture of PD at her school could help Lillian create the vantage she needs. Perhaps she can learn to see her problem of practice with new eyes in a way that helps her shift her perspective. To test this belief, let's approach Lillian's potential through the lens of the Headwinds and Beacons.

Lillian's Journey at the Headwinds School

Left to her own devices and facing the Headwinds of the status quo on her Island of Practice, what might Lillian experience on her professional journey?

FURTHER LEARNING

These questions come from Freakonomics podcast, Episode 379: "How to Change Your Mind?" It's well worth the listen and will enrich your understanding of some of the research that supports our journey.

A *Math Talk* (sometimes called a Number Talk or an Algebra Talk) is an instructional routine where students discuss different ways to mentally solve a problem. The focus is on students making mathematical connections between different solution methods.

Someone *other than Lillian* decides that Math Talks should be taught often and dedicates time in their "PD calendar" to "train" teachers how to deliver them. But depending on Lillian's mindset, this top-down approach may seem like just another mandate, something that is followed out of a duty of compliance rather than pursued with the enthusiasm of belief. Maybe she's fed up with the endless sequence of disjointed "quick-fix" strategies that don't help her achieve her vision of equity. And she may not see Math Talks as a more productive action than what she's currently doing.

Lillian's takeaway might be, *Why is admin wasting my time in another PD that doesn't help me get my kids ready?*

Perhaps she never gets this PD at all because the benefits of Math Talks aren't valued by local leadership. They may prefer instead to spend PD time looking at student assessment data and making a strategic instructional plan to get students "ready" for this year's test. This action certainly won't help Lillian get unstuck *because she's doing that already*. Her current PD may actually validate her own confirmation bias and motivate her to follow a pathway that will lead to *less* professional flourishment.

Something Lillian may say to us as a colleague in this PD, *You see here? Only 23% of my students got this question right. I'm going to need to reteach them how to do that. Ugh. Why didn't they learn this last year?*

Maybe the top-down PD is delivered effectively. All the teachers give positive feedback and leadership thinks that teachers have everything they need to be successful at implementing Math Talks in their lessons. But they are puzzled when, a month later, only a handful of teachers report having tried them more than once or twice.

Leaders may tell themselves, *We've given them all the ingredients they need for success. Why can't they just put the recipe together?* Perhaps they even say, *Some of our teachers, like Lillian, must not have that teaching gift.*

In response, the school leaders ratchet up accountability tools, walking through teacher's classrooms collecting data on clipboards—data that still won't tell Lillian how to get better at her craft of delivering Math Talks. Nor will this change her beliefs about her current actions. It may even make her feel shamed because she doesn't have the "knack for it" like her colleagues do.

She may tell herself, *I hope admin doesn't come in after lunch. Those are my worst classes. What will they think of me? Why are they even here anyway? I feel judged.*

We operate in a system of silos.

Regardless of Lillian's reaction to the PD or the quality of it, she's still going to go back to her classroom, close the door, and whatever she does, she will most likely do it alone in her silo.

Phew. Glad that's over. Now I'm back in my space with my system. I'm in control. Let's get back to teaching those basics!

I'm sure that Lillian, at some point, gains the vantage she needs to change her course of action. But given the contexts of these Headwinds, it doesn't seem like PD will be of much help, does it? And when she does eventually get unstuck, I'm also sure that Lillian wished she had gotten unstuck sooner—saying what we all say after we finally admit that what we believe isn't as true as we once thought: *Why did I waste so much time doing that when I could've been doing this instead?*

Earlier, I invited you to think about something you used to believe about math teaching, but no longer do and what it took to change your mind. *Well, what would it have taken to change your mind sooner?* Because somewhere out there in your future is a version of yourself telling you *right now* that you need to create some vantage on something—a belief or an action—that's not as productive as you currently think it is. You just don't see it yet. That's one of the key points of deliberate practice and the role of vantage—learning how to see what we need to see sooner so we can maximize our growth in the moment and over the arc of our careers.

> That's one of the key points of deliberate practice and the role of vantage-learning how to see what we need to see sooner so we can maximize our growth in the moment and over the arc of our careers.

Lillian's Journey at the Beacons School

Now, let's imagine for a moment that Lillian works in a professional culture that follows the Beacons. What might her journey for more professional flourishment look like under these conditions? How might she get the vantage she needs sooner?

Our efforts to transform must come from the "inside-out."

Lillian works at a school where teachers are viewed as passionate professionals who are valued for their expertise. Leadership invests time in establishing a culture of PD that enhances the identities of their teachers in ways that foster each of their senses of agencies. She and her colleagues feel empowered to take ownership of their own professional learning, and the administrators work hard to remove obstacles, provide the resources, and offer teachers the PD time they need. Everybody sees themselves as lifelong learners—as unfinished educators who are still finding ways to improve their expertise. A large poster in the faculty room says, "Step 0 of the learning process is being comfortable with not knowing."

In this culture, Lillian might tell herself, *I still don't think Math Talks are for me or my students. But I've changed my mind about things before. I'm open.*

Motivation is fostered most when we calibrate our measures to our values.

At Lillian's school, the community talks extensively about what they value and the language and measures they use to evaluate the effectiveness of their work. Knowing that assessment data only offers a narrow glimpse into a student's brilliance, Math Talks are presented to teachers as a productive action for furthering the math stories for all students—regardless of their current "level of proficiency."

Lillian is positioned in a way that she can stop and ask herself, *Hmm. Math Talks could help me get my struggling learners ready, but what would my stronger students get out of it? They already know the algorithms. Isn't this stuff beneath them?*

We must continually seek vantage, particularly from the students' perspective.

Lillian's professional schedule allows her an hour a week to sit in on her colleague's math lessons and seek a new perspective on how Math Talks can be a more productive way to review skills than her typical crash course on "the basics"—particularly from the student perspective. She's more likely to see that the actions she has been undertaking are having an unproductive impact on their math identities and their sense of agency. She might see that she's making them *less ready* for future math classes because she's robbing them not only of the time they need to learn grade-level content but also of the chance to author the math stories they'll need to be successful beyond Lillian's class.

Maybe what I'm doing really isn't working. I'm not getting my kids ready when I do my review because I'm missing out on so much other content. And these Math Talks ... they get kids talking to each other. Even the stronger students seem to be engaged and learning. I can't get my kids talking like that about my worksheets. But I don't know. These Math Talks seem really different from my natural teaching style. This is going to be really awkward for me at first.

Effective math teaching is a craft we can study best through each other.

Colleagues regularly sit in on Lillian's classes too. Seeing her teach is helping them learn. Even Lillian's students benefit—they now see teachers as learners. And the classroom becomes a space for observation, study, and productive feedback. And in this culture of professionalism where all teachers feel that their professional learning is enhancing their identity, Lillian's colleagues are able to leverage their relationships to help her create the vantage she needs as active partners on their journey to flourishment.

I'm getting better at these Math Talks, but they're still not going as well as I would like. I wonder what missed opportunities my colleagues see from their position in the room. Maybe they can help me see what I could be doing better.

Sounds like an awesome place to work, right? Do you know any schools that are like this? I hope you do, but in my experience, it is extremely rare. I only know of one school where this culture of professionalism is the norm. So odds are, Lillian doesn't work in a "Beacons School." If she did, she would've changed her actions already and gotten unstuck.

FURTHER LEARNING

I invite you to check out the Eagle Rock School and Center for Professional Development in Estes Park, Colorado, at eaglerockschool. org. They are the Beacons embodied, and they welcome visitors like you.

What If Lillian Was on the Journey With Us?

Here's where I want to ask an essential question: What if Lillian was on a journey to professional flourishment with us? How might she find the vantage she needs—and find it sooner?

Again, what we can say to Lillian will be limited by the relationship we have with her. And despite the best of relationships, sometimes it's not helpful to tell people things they need to come to understand for themselves. Our invitation to collaborate on Math Talks may not be accepted, and then what? Lillian's still stuck and now she's just rejected our help, perhaps making us more reluctant to offer help in the future.

But if we had an established culture of deliberate practice with her, *our invitation becomes unnecessary.* By authentically engaging in deliberate practice with Lillian (and Lillian engaging authentically with us), she can create the vantage *she needs to change her own mind.* And when she does, she's ready to prune her Tree so she can start incorporating more productive actions into her teaching craft sooner.

Usis: It's What You Get When You Spell Sisu Backward

LANGUAGE NOTE

We won't use "usis" on our journey, but you might find it useful language for you and your colleagues.

Imagine being an ant, walking around on the surface of an orange, looking for a way to get off that orange. To monitor your progress, you put black paint on your feet. The first few times you cross your tracks, you're a bit discouraged. *Hmmm. I've been here before, but the way off of this orange has to be here somewhere.* Eventually, you cover the whole orange black. And you still haven't improved your position or improved the vantage on your position. But you keep going anyway, denying the obvious evidence right beneath your feet that you will never get off the orange by walking around.

Without vantage, it's hard to test beliefs and question actions. And the only difference between us and that ant? The ability to shift vantage—so long as we're not too stubborn.

There is a very wide line between what I mean by "sisu" and good ol' fashioned *"willful stubbornness."* It is a line that is very easy to see in others, like you might in Lillian, but it can be very difficult to see in ourselves. Sisu is about having resolve against the Immovable Mountains and the forces that do the most harm to the math stories of our students. Sisu is a type of resolve that *enhances our identity*. Willful stubbornness is having a refusal to admit that what we're doing isn't working. It's not sisu and a measure of our resolve—it's *the ego* and a measure of our mule-headed inflexibility. I like to call it *usis* because it's what we get when we spell sisu backward.

> *Sisu is about having resolve against the Immovable Mountains and the forces that do the most harm to the math stories of our students.*

How do you know the difference between sisu and usis? Vantage. How do we create vantage for ourselves on our own Tree? Now that is a question worth asking. And it's what I'm trying to show you in Part 2 of our journey.

In Our Own Way, We Are All Lillians

We're all hung up about *something*. Our Trees are symbols of our brilliant source of energy that we channel into giving students what they need. But as I've said before, our Trees are also very stubborn. We are biased toward our own beliefs—even the unproductive ones that are getting in our own way. In part, this is because it's simply the natural default setting we all have in our human brain. Deliberate practice is about remembering that and having the courage to change that default setting from saying *My actions are productive. My beliefs are accurate.* And start asking ourselves, *What's really going on here? What might I not know yet? What or whose perspective am I missing? How might my thinking be inaccurate or incomplete?*

It takes courage to ask these questions because questioning our actions requires us to admit that we might be wrong about our beliefs. And admitting we're wrong is *uncomfortable* work. It's uncomfortable to admit that there are so many things that we might not know. We've worked hard to build our wisdom and our teaching practice over the years. Our Tree got us to where we are, after all. Why would we prune back branches we've spent so much effort growing?

If you feel like I'm calling you out and saying you're wrong about some of your current beliefs, I'm not. That's a good way to make your ears get small. I'm saying that your future "teaching self" is calling you out about something your current "teaching self" believes right now—something that isn't as true as you currently believe it to be *and you don't see it yet*. And until you create the vantage you need, that unproductive belief will remain tacit to you. In fewer words, your Future Tree is telling you how your Existing Tree needs to be pruned so you can get busy thriving how your students need you to thrive.

I'm betting that if you let those words in, you know that I'm right.

How many times in your teaching life have you gone too far down a dead-end path and wished you had turned around sooner? We all have. But what if that's you, me, or your colleague right now? Individually and collectively, how do we create the vantage we need to see our dead ends sooner? And how do we do that for each other in ways that enhance our identities and foster our sense of agency?

This whole book is my offering on how we can answer these questions together.

Expanding Our Potential Means Pruning Our Tree

Remember the first Beacon. Your ability to remain an unfinished math teacher is dependent on your willingness to admit you're imperfect. Ask yourself, honestly, what do you want your Future Tree to look like in the years to come? Do you want it to be scarred with dead branches hanging off it—malnourished roots twisted around expectations that didn't come true? Do you want to have the same exact Tree you have now, whatever that may be? Or do you want your Tree to *continually* thrive and become more robust, to sustain its flourishment with the resilience of new branches growing outward because you have the courage to prune the unproductive limbs out of the way?

If you're still reading, I'm assuming you want this Tree of Flourishment. Expanding your potential necessitates pruning your Tree. It's the only way you can grow your expertise. As we journey forward, I invite you to keep looking at your professional identity with new eyes. Have the courage to create the vantage you need to actively seek out the unproductive beliefs that may currently be tacit to you. You've already pruned your Tree over your career—many times. Our journey is about creating the vantage we need to do that more regularly—so we can increase the efficiency of our efficacy by pruning away beliefs and actions that don't work for us—or our students.

KEY TAKEAWAYS FROM CHAPTER 4

* Creating internal vantage to test our beliefs and interrogate our actions is challenging because we, like all humans, want to believe we're right. We must shift our vantage and actively seek out unproductive loops of confirmation bias—examples of existing beliefs and current courses of actions that aren't productive for us but are still, at the moment, *tacit* to us.

* It is hard to create the vantage we need in the Headwinds because we are denied the opportunity to see what we need to see for ourselves.

* The Beacons, combined with the Core Elements of Deliberate Practice, offer us a pathway to position ourselves in ways that we can gain the vantage we need. When we create opportunities for vantage, we are creating space to test our beliefs and question our actions.

INTERLUDE 4:
WHAT IS YOUR TEACHING STORY?

Your journey as a teacher began before you picked up this book. Perhaps you're learning to survive the job as a new teacher, developing and improving your established practice as a seasoned teacher, or polishing your craft as a master teacher. Perhaps you've worked in many different types of schools, or you've spent your whole career dedicated to one school community. It's also possible that teaching is your second (or even third) career. While you bring a lot of life experiences to your work, your teaching craft is still forming and growing.

Regardless of your experience, we all have a teaching story and yours is unique. Thinking about and sharing our teaching story is a good place to start practicing the type of relationship building we need to engage in throughout our journey. You will use what you write in this Lighthouse Reflection as "fuel" to focus our conversation during the Campfire Gathering 1 below.

LIGHTHOUSE REFLECTION 1: WHAT IS YOUR TEACHING STORY?

FOCUS

Spend some time thinking deliberately about your journey as a teacher so far and how you got *right here* professionally.

- What is your teaching story?

To help you answer this question, consider any of the following questions. Or choose your own approach. Above all, be authentically you. You can write complete sentences, make a bullet-point list, create a map, or draw images for your answers. Again, these questions are only suggestions to help jump-start your thinking.

- What are some of the key moments in your professional journey that are significant to you? What unexpected twists have you navigated?

- How has your Vision of Equity changed over the years? What is something that you used to believe was true about effective math teaching, but no longer do? *What did it take to change your mind?*

- When did you know that you wanted to become a teacher? If you are a single-subject math teacher, why did you choose to teach mathematics (as opposed to other subjects)? What choice did you have in your teaching assignment (grade level, subject, location, etc.)?

- Where do you want your teaching story to go from here? When you think about yourself in five years, what do you want to be able to say about your work? What do you want your teaching legacy to be?

SEEK VANTAGE 1: NEW EYES ON YOUR ISLAND OF PRACTICE

VANTAGE

Finding vantage in a silo is like wading out in the ocean to try and see your whole Island of Practice. You can't get far enough away to gain the perspective you need. Hence, the boat icon—you actually have to get off your Island and travel to other landscapes in order to see your own with new eyes.

It may be uncomfortable at first, but the process will normalize over time for you, your colleagues, and the students in the room. Students are used to the silos of school too. They're not accustomed to teachers learning from each other in this way.

This is no small point. When we sit in on each other's classes, we are creating explicit data to our students that says, from their vantage, *Teachers are learners too. And they are learning because they care about what they do— they care about me.* Simply by doing this action, you are changing the math stories that are being authored in productive ways. *Your presence alone builds equity into the room.* Think about how the authority shifts when they see a teacher sitting next to them and learning with them. If you get nothing out of this activity, the students did.

The students are always watching.

> *When we sit in on each other's classes, we are creating explicit data to our students that says, from their vantage, Teachers are learners too. And they are learning because they care about what they do–they care about me.*

Before your first Campfire Gathering, spend time in each other's classrooms watching the teaching and learning of mathematics.

Here are some questions to think about before, during, and after the observations to help focus your learning.

Before the observation(s): Reflect on the existing state of your Island of Practice.

- How's math teaching going for you right now? What are some things that are going well in your classroom? What are some things that you might like to change?

- What are some challenges you want to learn to navigate better in your classroom?

- How might this experience create vantage for you and help you learn more about what's going on in your Garden?

During the observation(s): Look/Listen/Feel

- Pay attention to all the sources of data you have access to. What do you see? What do you hear? What does the energy feel like?
- What does the data tell you about students' math identity? Their agency?
- What does the data tell you about the math stories being authored? How does the data you're seeing compare with the data in your own Garden?

At the end of observation(s): Engage in 2 minutes of relationship building.

- Observer identifies some valuable data and new learning by finishing any (or all) of the following sentences. Remember, the language we use is an opportunity to position each other in ways that we can be active partners in each other's growth. Seek Vantage is about the observers learning about themselves.

  "Something that really impressed me *and why* ..."

  "Something I'm wondering about my own Garden is ..."

  "Something I'm considering doing/applying in my own Garden tomorrow/this week is ..."

After the observation(s): Take a pause and reflect on your experience.

- What teacher actions did you observe that make you think more deeply about your own actions in your Garden?
- What student data did you observe that makes you think more deeply about the student data you're seeing in your Garden?
- What new eyes do you have on your Island of Practice? How might that new learning affect your teaching practice? What might you consider doing differently for your Garden?

A Few Words About Campfire Gatherings

Relationships are all there is. Everything in the universe only exists because it is in relationship to everything else. Nothing exists in isolation. We have to stop pretending we are individuals who can go it alone.

—*Wheatley (2002)*

You're invited to conduct your first Campfire Gathering, and I'd like to offer a few more words about the purpose of these activities before we start.

- When we talk about what we have in common, we create space for more authentic opportunities to connect with others and build rapport and understanding—the foundations for a culture of safety and inclusion that allow us to be vulnerable about our struggles in the classroom. Placing blame and debating who is right or wrong are not the reasons we are taking our journey. Instead, our journey is about creating a different story for ourselves as teachers of mathematics, a different narrative about how we grow and develop our craft of math teaching. Our purpose in Campfire Gatherings is to transcend much of the debate that divides us and *find common truths about our work teaching mathematics* so that we can achieve more professional flourishment *for ourselves* as active partners in each other's growth.

> *Our purpose in Campfire Gatherings is to transcend much of the debate that divides us and find common truths about our work teaching mathematics so that we can achieve more professional flourishment for ourselves as active partners in each other's growth.*

These conversations are *listening* activities where our primary focus is to help others feel heard. We will do this by deliberately mirroring back and paraphrasing what we hear others saying.

When we feel heard, several things happen. First, we foster an appreciation for each other's professional identity and the journey they are on. Second, we strengthen our relationships by deepening our trust in each other—trust that we won't be judged for being the imperfect, unfinished math teachers we are. Third, when we listen to others, we can learn about ourselves and our own thinking. For example, you may find yourself saying, *I've never thought about it that way before.* Last, when others reflect back what they hear us say, we get the benefit of hearing our own thinking. This vantage can help us more clearly "see" our own beliefs.

- If you have a coach to help facilitate these conversations, that may be helpful. But I've written agendas for you to follow because I believe that you have the capacity to facilitate these for yourselves. Think of these Gatherings like "talking circles" or "council" or the other structured discourse activities you may have conducted in advisory or participated in elsewhere during your career.

- Please do not try to reduce these agendas down to a checklist. There are no checklists in this book. As you evolve as a group of colleagues learning how to be active partners in each other's growth, you may find other discourse strategies that you can add to these agendas yourself. I've simply chosen the ones that are low-floor and high-leverage for you to start with.

- As you participate, I invite you to set aside a desire to solve, fix, or rescue your colleague or to reply with your own autobiographical anecdote that you think relates. Your job is to listen and mirror back. Simply get to know each other.

- Avoid sarcasm. This is not a time for teasing. We may think we know what's in each other's Sea of Shame, but we don't.

- Although you might find these Gatherings cathartic, this is not therapy. Everyone here is sharing only what they feel comfortable sharing. A culture of consent is always essential. Set aside your desire to ask probing questions of each other, for now. We will learn how to do this for each other in Part 3 of our journey. 🔥

CAMPFIRE GATHERING AGENDA 1: SHARE YOUR TEACHING STORIES.

RELATIONSHIPS

Purpose: To practice enhancing each other's identity by mirroring back what we hear.

At this gathering, you'll each have about 5-7 minutes of uninterrupted time to share your teaching story with each other. To prepare, look at your notes from "Lighthouse Reflection 1: What Is Your Teaching Story?"

What parts of your teaching story seem most significant to share? What do you want others to know about your professional journey? 🔥

NOTES

_____

_____

_____

_____

_____

_____

_____

_____

_____

_____

_____

_____

_____

_____

_____

_____

_____

_____

5

TEACHING IS A CULTURAL ACTIVITY

Where We've Been

In Chapter 4, we looked through a window together into Lillian's classroom. We examined how vantage helps us see what we need to see for ourselves when we find ourselves stuck. Unfortunately, creating internal vantage to test our beliefs and question our actions is challenging because we, like all humans, want to believe we're right.

Where We're Going

In Chapter 5, we will see how teaching is a cultural activity—it is something we learn through our participation in schools. It can be difficult to create vantage on our cultural beliefs because they are often deeply rooted in our psyche and remain untested. They are often *unseen*, but we need to make them seen. In this chapter, you will also continue to engage in the Core Elements of Deliberate Practice as you build your capacity to become active partners in each other's professional growth by talking about your own math story with each other.

Teaching, in our view, is a cultural activity . . . .
This might be surprising, because teaching is
rarely thought of in this way . . . some people
think that teaching is an innate skill, something
you are born with. Others think that teachers
learn to teach by enrolling in college teacher-
training programs. We believe that neither
is the best description. Teaching, like other
cultural activities, is learned through informal

participation over long periods of time. It is something one learns to do more by growing up in a culture than by studying it formally.

—Stigler and Hiebert, *The Teaching Gap* (1999, p. 86)

My Math Story

I share my math story so you can know a bit more about my lived experience as a student and to show you how heavily programmed we can become by the school system when it comes to our personal beliefs about "math class" and what it means to be "good at math." As you read my story, I invite you to look for moments when my beliefs about who I was informed my actions as a student—and how those actions created data that reinforced my existing beliefs.

I also share my math story so you understand what we mean when we say that teaching is a cultural activity. "Math class" is something we learn tacitly through our lived experience as students. In order to change how we teach, we must bring these tacit values to the surface so we can test and interrogate the beliefs that we carry with us from our math stories as students. Our expertise at achieving equitable outcomes as math teachers is always going to be dependent on the cultural programming we need to undo from our experiences as a math student.

In my math story, I use quotation marks around course titles and other terms that are jargon at this point. I took "Algebra 1 Honors" in eighth grade in 1989. I don't want us to presume that we have a common understanding about what that means. When I was a senior in high school, "AP (Advanced Placement) Calculus" was the pinnacle course for most "college-bound" students. Nowadays, the bar has been raised so high that "college-bound" students accelerate their math classes to a degree that was not the norm when I graduated high school in 1994. At that time, my "3.78 GPA" was good enough for top-10 in my graduating class of 160. Nowadays, a "3.78 GPA" is a much lower ranking.

Throughout my math story—and throughout this book—I will mention some "twists of fate." Our journeys often hinge on these little twists of fate—the coincidences and circumstances that ultimately change our course through life. We are often the way we are, not because we were born that way, but because of how we learned to survive and thrive early on in our lives as children. For example, I was an only child raised by a single mother who was an officer in the U.S. Air Force. We moved around a lot—Washington State, England, Norway, Florida, New Hampshire. If you were a military brat like me, you know what it was like to move every few years—new town, new friends, new school—*new eyes*. It gives you a lot of vantage growing up. Experiencing all this vantage as a young child accelerated my thinking about schools simply because I was in a position to see that there was more than one way to do school.

When I started fifth grade, life became more rooted, and I was fortunate to live in the same town in southern New Hampshire for eight years, fifth grade through twelfth grade. We lived on the middle-class side of an upper-middle-class town. The school system was considered "excellent" and was well-funded by an affluent tax base. About 95% of my classmates were white, like me.

My Math Story: First Grade to Tenth Grade, 1982-1992

My first vivid memory in math class was when I was six. I remember figuring out conceptually using pictures, why two odd numbers, when added together, make an even. It was my first moment loving math. I remember feeling *very* accomplished. *Look what I figured out!*

My next clear memory is in fourth grade—long division. It was the first time that math became an algorithm to follow rather than something that was supposed to be understood. I remember the teacher saying that she was *going to need to walk us through it, and it would take a lot of practice.* I remember sensing that she was nervous about teaching it. It was the first time I saw a teacher display self-doubt. *Woah, this long division thing must be hard stuff.*

In fourth grade, I also took a "bubble test" to see if I was "talented and gifted." The test told me that I was at an eighth grade level in mathematics. But I was only at a fifth grade level when it came to reading and writing. The test told me that I wasn't good enough to be labeled as "talented and gifted." I was whatever everybody else was. Normal? Average? Regular? Ordinary? (Seven years later, my SAT scores would reflect the same story. "720" mathematics, "470" verbal. Still not "talented and gifted"—at least not enough for the "Tier 1" colleges my peers were getting accepted to.)

My next memory is seventh grade. We were invited to complete 50 Quests throughout the year. These were optional worksheets that focused on enrichment skills to prepare us to jump into the "honors track" for eighth grade "Algebra 1"—setting me on that all-important pathway to the pinnacle of math: a mysterious class called "AP Calculus." If I did my work, I would one day get to learn this elite math. I was told it would make my future high school transcript look good for college. I remember enjoying seeing my progress on the chart on the back wall as I put stickers for each Quest I completed. I remember learning how to write numbers in base-2, base-8, and base-16 and liking the Quest problems more than the problems in my textbook. Quests challenged me to think about mathematics in interesting ways. *Why aren't we all doing this type of math?*

"Algebra 1 Honors" went fine in eighth grade. I remember being really confused by the quadratic formula. *Why does it exist? Why is it so weird and ugly?* I remember learning to sing the song to memorize it and learning when to use it, but I didn't *understand* it. (It wasn't until my first year of teaching, as a 24-year-old adult, when I spent an hour after school deriving the proof myself that I truly understood the quadratic formula.)

In high school, I remember they had a machine shop and offered auto mechanic classes and other hands-on "trade-tech" courses. They were in a different part of the school, but happened to be next door to my "Geometry Honors" class. I would peek in and see rotors and engines and gears and tools all over the tables. *This looks fun. Students do stuff in here.* I wanted to be in that class, but I remember telling myself: *Students like me aren't supposed to take classes like "auto shop." I'm going to college.*

I didn't like geometry because of all the proofs. I remember in the spring term that there were too many theorems for me to memorize and hold in my mind. *This stack of flashcards is getting too big.* I remember being relieved when the course was over and I didn't have to keep all that memorized. (I still have hesitant emotions when it comes to teaching or solving geometry tasks as an adult.)

In 10th grade, "Algebra 2 Honors," I remember being at the chalkboard with my classmate Kelly. We were each given a problem to solve while the teacher walked around and checked homework. It was a part of the classroom routine that I had come to expect over the years. *This is the way math class goes.* I don't remember what the problem was. Something about conic sections. I was clueless. So was Kelly. We looked at each other. I asked her if she had any ideas. She shrugged. So we started whispering to each other about how we might solve it— until the teacher *bellowed* from the back of the classroom. *CHEATERS! Back to your seats. ZEROS for both of you!* I put my head down so my classmates wouldn't see the tears. It stayed down that whole class.

Continued →

→ Continued

I dreaded not Algebra 2, but *his* class. I failed the midterm at the end of the first semester. In a dark twist of fate, that teacher had a heart attack two weeks into second semester. He survived, but at 63, he never returned to the classroom. Our new teacher was kinder. Class was still hard, but at least the emotional dread was gone. I think I got a B.

Looking Through the Window: What I Learned After 10 Years of Math Class

Although most people have not studied to be teachers, most people have been students. People within a culture share a mental picture of what teaching is like. We call this mental picture a *script* … . Cultural activities, such as teaching, are not invented full-blown but rather evolve over long periods of time in ways that are consistent with the stable web of beliefs and assumptions that are part of the culture.

—Stigler and Hiebert, *The Teaching Gap* (1999, pp. 86-87)

Going into my junior year, the list below represents my beliefs about math class, mathematics, and my own math identity. None of this was explicitly told to me. That's the thing about cultural activities—there's a lot of conditioning going on below the surface we're not aware of. And our journey requires us to bring that to the surface so we can gain more vantage on our own unproductive beliefs and actions and the unproductive story making that is happening in our Gardens.

Math class is best set up with rows of desks—five rows of six seems to be the favored formation.

Every year, I sat at one of these desks—my own "assigned seat"—by myself. Never in these 10 years of math class do I remember ever sitting in a group or with a partner. Other than asking a classmate to see if we got the same answers, I don't have any memories of meaningfully engaging in mathematical thinking with another classmate.

Math class follows a script.

We come in. Attendance is taken. Homework is checked or collected. New problems are explained. We copy them down as "notes" and practice the "notetaking skills" we will need in "college classes." We practice problems in class until the end of the period. Then we finish the rest for homework. This script repeats until we begin a review for the "chapter test." We take that test. A few days later, after we've started another chapter, we get our tests back with a score on it. Good students like me put the tests in our binders in case we need them to study for the final later in the year. Others would throw them in the trash on the way out the door. *Why don't they care about their academics like I do?*

Over time, I became aware that this script worked for me, but not others. As a shy, awkward introvert, I was happy to sit quietly and take notes, and I was content doodling and daydreaming when I was bored. I simply figured out what the teacher needed of me, and I was rewarded with good grades for being compliant and studious. While I was fine playing the game of "math class," I saw others with their heads down and quitting or disengaging—certainly not taking notes in their binders like a good math student is supposed to do. *Why aren't they trying anymore? Don't they know this matters on our transcripts?*

Math is a process to find right answers, and I'm good at it.

I enjoyed doing homework and checking my answers in the back of the book. It was a routine that I found nourishing because it validated my identity as being "good at math" and a "college-bound student."

Math class is about learning procedures—procedures my teacher knows, but I do not.

My job as a student was to listen and learn so I could reproduce various procedures with accuracy on a test. Conceptual understanding of mathematics wasn't something I remember being valued or assessed. While I could calculate operations with integers with ease and knew that "two negative signs in a row make a positive," I couldn't draw you a picture to show you why "-2 - (-5) = 3." (In fact, it wasn't until my 14th year as a math educator—*20 years later*—that a middle school teacher taught me about "zero pairs" and showed me how to use physical counters to show why this is true. *How did I make it this far as a high school math teacher without someone showing me this?* Remember, I was a 36-year-old adult at the time.)

Math problems are things we can solve quickly.

Up to that point in my student career, I had never spent more than 10 minutes on a math problem before either solving it or giving up and waiting for the teacher to show me how to do it.

Continued →

→ *Continued*

The purpose of a math course is to get ready for the next math course.

I completed the Quests so I would be ready for Algebra 1. I took Algebra 1 so I could be ready for Geometry. Geometry got me ready for Algebra 2. So on and so forth. In this way, mathematics, to me, was a continuous pathway that builds on itself—miss one link along the way, then you "fall behind" and risk not "being ready" for what's next.

I am an "A-" math student with "excellent" participation skills.

At the end of 10th grade, I had been a student in more than 1,800 math lessons. If you put all my work as a math student into one place, it would be a binder containing thousands of pages—all of it homework marked with "checks" and "check-plusses," notes with doodles, scored quizzes, and tests containing tens of thousands of short, simple routine math problems *that someone else showed me how to do.*

Scattered within this binder would be 10 report cards all with a letter next to a "math class." On average, these report cards say that my work is worth an "A-" and that my participation is "excellent"—even though I hardly ever talked in class.

Let's say that my math story ended there and that was all I ever knew about what a math class could look, sound, and feel like. It would be my only mental model—the only story I would be able to tell myself about how math class is supposed to go. And if I had gone into math teaching with this math story, that would be the math classroom I would have strived to create.

How equitable and inclusive would that classroom be?

Probably not very. It would have worked for students like me, but not for others. But that would have been my vision of equity nonetheless—until I gained the vantage to see that math class could be any different.

My Math Story Continued

My Math Story: Tenth Grade to Beginning of My Teaching Story, 1992-1995

By a fortunate twist of fate, the school district I attended school in had decided, years prior, to split into two. For decades, our three small New Hampshire towns were bonded together by a common high school. Now, after the completion of my sophomore year, we were separated into two high schools. Teammates became rivals.

My school happened to be the brand new one with a handpicked staff who believed in the 10 Common Principles of the Coalition of Essential Schools, principles such as "learning to use one's mind well" and "student-as-worker, teacher-as-coach." It was the first time in my public education that my thoughts, and the thoughts of my classmates, were regularly valued in the math classroom. Remember, I was a junior in high school by this time, a veteran of 1,800 math classes. *This is a better way to do school. Why haven't we been learning this way the whole time—not just in math class, but in all our classes?*

Thanks to Mr. Boz, my math story changed during my 11th and 12th grade years. I had him for both "Precalculus" and "AP Calculus." In these classes, the overall script was very similar to before. We still had a textbook. We still worked through problems, completed homework assignments, and took chapter tests.

Here's what was fundamentally different:

We had no assigned seats. *Uh-oh. I have to choose where I sit?*

We sat in groups. *Oh no! The introvert in me doesn't like this at all.*

We were encouraged to talk to each other. *I'm shy. Let me hide please. This is really awkward.*

The first few weeks in Mr. Boz's class were really challenging for me emotionally. I had never been in this position as a math student before—it challenged my math identity and what it meant to be good at math. But Mr. Boz was a caring teacher, and he clearly wanted to know what we were thinking. He set norms around how we talked to one another and how we treated each other as we learned how to elevate our own voice and foster our own sense of agency. We were given quiet think time to try problems on our own before we talked about them. It was also the first time I remember a teacher teaching me about the conceptual ideas within mathematics in addition to the procedures. *Maybe this way of doing math class isn't so bad after all.*

Continued →

→ *Continued*

I like the new relationship I'm having with math. I also like learning with my classmates.

Every now and again, he'd flip the script. He'd bring in a task for us to work on, and we'd spend the whole class figuring it out together and sharing solutions. It was the first time I ever worked on a single math problem for a whole class period. My favorite task was about the mathematical relationships between musical notes. The context brought a richness to mathematics—and to music—that I had never experienced before. *Math isn't just what we learn in textbooks. It's something out there … in the world … and it is worth wondering about. It's something that is discovered.*

In "AP Calculus," I gained an appreciation of math that I never experienced before. Continuity, limits, derivatives, integrals, the infinitely big and the infinitesimally small, *dividing by zero*—all concepts that tickled my brain and excited me. It was delicious. *Why did it take so long until we got to the good stuff?* I had usually felt validated in math class, but that didn't mean I really liked math or truly understood it. Mr. Boz's classes were the first time math made coherent sense to me beyond procedural algorithms. It was wonderful. And I wanted to learn more math.

It was an emotion that didn't last long.

The summer before college, as I chose my courses, I signed up for a math class because I thought *Well, I've always taken math before. Why would I stop now?* I signed up for a class called "Calculus III" because it was the recommended calculus course for students who received a "4" or "5" on the AP exam. I remember the roman numerals made it seem impressive in the course catalog. *I'm good enough for this class. And Calculus III seems like the next step in the sequence of math, right?* I had no one to advise me that mathematics didn't have to be learned in some sacred sequence. It simply never occurred to me that there might be other types of mathematics I might want to explore—even though they were listed *right there* in the course catalog I was holding in my hands. My mental model of what mathematics was had always been "Algebra 1 → Geometry → Algebra 2 → Precalculus → AP Calculus." Calculus III was the obvious choice.

There were about 25 students at the beginning of Calculus III. We had four exams—I got 96, 81, 66, and 51 on the final. I remember because the test scores went down 15 points each time. With all due respect to the dedicated and talented professors at Wheaton College in Norton, Massachusetts, who helped me grow as a person, this professor was a crappy teacher. He would talk at length on tangents that weren't related to the content we were expected to learn, and he actively showed contempt when we didn't do well on his tests. I only got the 96 because I had such a strong foundation from Mr. Boz's class the year before. At the end of the semester, the professor graded us on a curve because he'd "get in trouble if he failed too many of us." By that point, there were only 12 of us in class—more than half had dropped it. I got a B+.

It was the last math class I ever took in my life. I was 18 at the time.

My math story halted, I set off to take advantage of a liberal arts education and pursue my passions for astronomy, theater, religious studies, education, and eventually majored in English Literature. I made magna cum laude. I say this not to brag. I say this because it was a hard-earned and self-affirming *Eff You!* to the SAT and that stupid talented and gifted test from fourth grade.

From a Math Story to a Teaching Story

My Tree Takes Root

During the second semester of my first year of college, I had some friends taking "Calculus I" with the same math professor. Turns out, he was a really crappy teacher in their class too! My friends were stressed, *anxious*. It was the first time I heard the phrase "math anxiety." They needed to pass the class in order to major in the sciences. And they were failing. So I started tutoring. We'd go down in the basement of the library and find an office space with a whiteboard and work through problems together in groups, sometimes until 1:00 a.m.

Just a few months after my math story had come to an abrupt halt, my math teaching story was born—ironically all as a result of the same crappy teacher. Now, to say that I was *teaching* is a bit of a stretch. All I was doing was what was most familiar. *Let me show you how to do it. I will explain it to you until you can do it on your own. I'm here to help. Do you have any questions?* I was already beginning to reproduce the cultural script, positioning myself as the answer key.

Regardless, I was bitten by the teaching bug. I ended up tutoring math all through college, in part as a personal quest to undo the harm this crappy professor was causing on the math stories of my friends, but mostly because I enjoyed the hell out of it. It was my first taste of professional flourishment. *My Tree had taken root.*

Continued →

→ *Continued*

I learned a few valuable lessons about math teaching in those tutoring years:

- A crappy teacher can derail a productive math story in a heartbeat.

- Crappy math teaching becomes a social justice issue when we start blaming failures on students before taking a hard look at the quality of teaching that is being offered.

These lessons inspired me to minor in education. With the help of Professor Frinde Maher, I designed an independent study course. We met on Friday afternoons during my final semester to discuss Paulo Freire, bell hooks, Pierre Bourdieu, and others as we looked at the issue of "multiculturalism" in education and how schools are used in the machinery of society to reproduce socioeconomic inequalities. Armed with all this knowledge of "critical theory"—and all the naivete of a 22-year-old college kid, I went into math teaching convinced that I would be different, that I would change the system. *I will become the math teacher the world needs. How hard could it possibly be?*

What did I do once I started teaching in the math classroom? I hope you can guess the answer by now. I resorted to the same script I knew. *OK students. Watch me do these problems. Then you do them. And we'll just keep turning pages in our textbook until we get to the end of the chapter. And then we'll have a test. I'm here to help you out, and I'll show you how to do it. Even if you can't do it, I'll pass you if you try your best and don't give me a hard time, OK?*

All was not lost. At least I had my students sitting in groups and sharing their thoughts with one another. Thank god for Mr. Boz.

KEY TAKEAWAYS FROM CHAPTER 5

✳ Teaching is a cultural activity. Much of our mental model about "mathematics," "math class," and "math teaching" is informed from our experiences as students in school. Many of us start our teaching story replicating the experiences we had in our own classrooms.

✳ In order to further our expertise of achieving productive and equitable outcomes for more of our students in the classroom, we need to bring these tacit cultural beliefs to the surface so we can test them to see if they are productive to helping our students author an empowering math story.

✳ Crappy teaching can ruin a math story in a heartbeat. Crappy teaching is also a social justice issue when we start blaming students for the failures of teachers and the system we work in.

INTERLUDE 5:
WHAT IS YOUR MATH STORY?

LIGHTHOUSE REFLECTION 2: WHAT IS YOUR MATH STORY?

FOCUS

Spend a moment reflecting on your own experiences in math class as a student in school, before you ever became a teacher.

- What is your math story?

- What did math class teach you about your math identity and abilities as a mathematical thinker? Did you identify as "being good at math"?

- How was math taught to you as a student? What was valued by your teachers? What did it mean to be a "good math student" in their classrooms?

Now look at your beliefs with "new eyes."

- How might your personal math story influence your current beliefs about yourself as a professional teacher of mathematics?

- How do the math classes you had as a student compare with the math class you've created for your students?

- How might your personal math story be affecting your decisions in the classroom as you help your students author a productive math story for themselves? ❧

SEEK VANTAGE 2: NEW EYES ON OUR ACTIONS

VANTAGE

Our second Seek Vantage will look much like the first. Some of these questions are similar, some ask you to focus more keenly on the teacher's actions from the student's perspective. What math story are they authoring?

In the next few days, I invite you to spend time in each other's classrooms observing math class from the teaching and learning of mathematics thinking about "math class" from the students' perspective.

Here are some questions to think about before, during, and after the observations to help focus your learning.

Before the observation(s): Reflect on your vision of equity and the math stories you want your students to author. You may want to revisit your notes from Interlude 3:

Your Vision of Equity

- Think about your math lessons from the students' perspective. What data are they seeing/hearing/feeling in your Garden? What math story are you trying to help them author?

During the observation(s): Sit in the classroom and pretend you're a student. Look/Listen/Feel.

- What are they seeing/hearing/feeling—from their perspective? What math stories might they be making?

- What do students seem to value most? What incentives are motivating them?

- How is authority shared in the room? What missed opportunities do you notice where students' voice could be elevated more?

- What actions do you see the teacher make that make you question your own actions?

At the end of observation(s): Engage in 2 minutes of relationship building. See prompts in Seek Vantage 1 in Interlude 4.

After the observation(s): Before continuing your journey, take a pause and reflect on your experience.

- What teacher actions did you observe that make you think more deeply about your own actions in your Garden?

- What student data did you observe that makes you think more deeply about the student data you're seeing in your Garden?

- What new eyes do you have on your own actions? How might that new learning affect your teaching practice? What might you consider doing differently for your Garden?

CAMPFIRE GATHERING AGENDA 2: SHARE YOUR MATH STORIES

RELATIONSHIPS

You're invited to conduct your second Campfire Gathering. As you prepare for this gathering, it may be useful to refer back to the agenda from our first Campfire Gathering in Interlude 4 to remind yourselves how to facilitate these activities. This gathering will flow much like the previous one.

Purpose: To value each other's lived experience as students in math class.

At this gathering, you'll each have about 5-7 minutes of uninterrupted time to share your math story with each other. To prepare, look at your notes from "Lighthouse Reflection 2: What Is Your Math Story?"

What parts of your math story seem most significant to share? What do you want others to know about your journey as a student in math class? ●

6

CRAVING NOURISHMENT

Where We've Been

In Chapter 5, we saw how teaching is a cultural activity—it is something we learn tacitly by our participation in schools. It can be difficult to create vantage for ourselves when it comes to our own cultural beliefs. They are often deeply rooted and remain untested because they are often unseen.

Where We're Going

In Chapter 6, we will continue to define and give meaning to the Tree as we explore the passions we bring to our work and what nourishes us the most as teachers.

Talking About My Tree

In Chapters 6 and 7, I'm going to share some stories about my Tree, and I want to say a few things before I do.

▶ I share these stories so you know me. You have a right to know what passions nourish me as a teacher because, as I'll share in the next chapter, my Tree is biased toward those passions. I want to position you in a way to more readily see the biases that my lived experiences bring to this book so I can be a more productive window for you in the chapters to come.

▶ I share these stories because I trust you won't judge me. Just like I trust you not to judge each other when you talk in your

"Mirroring Conversations" about the moments that matter most to your teaching soul. I want to model that for you by sharing some of the most difficult moments from my own teaching story as if I was your colleague sitting in the circle with you.

➤ Please know I'm not a tortured, disgruntled former math teacher. I only have so many pages to shape our journey, and I want to pick the windows that potentially have the most impact, the most value to you. Because these are moments when I'm lacking wholeness and find myself awash in my own Sea of Shame, I simply don't have the *authority* to create a Lillian or a LeRon to say these things. I can't speak for the *emotions and identity* of others. I can only speak for my own Tree. Same for you.

Besides, you don't *really* want to read about the times my Tree felt the most brilliant, do you? My hunch is that you want to know the times when my Tree was most challenged, troubled, and *unnourished*—and how I learned to grow it back. So here are a few windows into some of the more visceral moments of my career when my flourishment was at its lowest.

It's Hard to See Yourself When You're Moving at the Speed of School

Teaching, like any truly human activity, emerges from one's inwardness, for better or worse. *As I teach, I project the condition of my soul onto my students, my subject, and our way of being together.* The entanglements I experience in the classroom are often no more or less than the convolutions of my inner life. Viewed from this angle, teaching holds a mirror to the soul. If I am willing to look in that mirror and not run from what I see, I have the chance to gain self knowledge—and knowing myself is as crucial to good teaching as knowing my students and my subject.

—Palmer, *Courage to Teach* (1998, p. 2; emphasis mine)

YOUR TEACHING NIGHTMARE

RELATIONSHIPS

What is your teaching nightmare in one word? Mine is "boredom."

What happens to you when that nightmare comes true and you actually see it happening in your own classroom? How do you feel? How do you react? ●

List the things we have to go through every teaching day, and you'll understand why we need nourishment from our work. I mean, can we talk for a moment about how demanding, exacting, and formidable—how outright *exhausting*—the job of teaching really is?

The life of a teacher is a life of being overworked and underpaid, of long nights, short sleeps, and early mornings. It's germs and fatigue and getting sick on the first day of vacation because your body gave every last ounce of itself to your students. A teacher's life is giving snacks to students we know don't have enough to eat and keeping a toiletry kit in our desk drawer for a student who's living out of a car—and keeping it all hidden from their classmates because you respect their dignity. It's helping young people grow up in a world that is vastly different from the one we grew up in. Fire drills turned into active shooter drills. The rumor mill turned from graffiti on bathroom stalls to posts on the internet walls. Snow days, natural disasters, and national tragedies closed our school doors for a few days. They've had—in a sense—more than a year of their childhoods cancelled by a pandemic.

Every single day we must fluidly navigate the legitimate trauma and the immature drama of young people and try to choreograph that into a productive learning experience in the math classroom. Our sense of fatigue worsens as we have to spend time and energy doing stuff that doesn't align with our purpose. There are countless distractions that interfere with our ability to meet students with the love, understanding, and *grace* they deserve. The "digital paperwork" demands attendance, grading, and photocopying, and discipline. And emails—always more emails. The lesson planning and the meetings and monitoring lunch, recess, and hallways during passing periods. Tolerating technology failures, unexpected assemblies, poorly organized pep rallies, and an endless assault of interruptions over the intercom speaker. District politics, school politics, department politics, and the unproductive debates and power grabs. Concerned parents, helicopter parents, and absent parents. Language learners, learners with Individualized Education Programs, and learners whose challenges aren't even diagnosed yet. *How am I supposed to meet all these needs?*

We have to do this juggling act at the pace of school under the watchful eye of the ticking clock; and we know, in our heart of hearts, that we are behind schedule in our Gardens and feel the need to rush to catch up. The district pacing plan always seems to move faster than the pace of student learning.

Effective Teaching Requires Authenticity

I invite you to name a job that demands the same degree of authenticity and self-knowledge as teaching. I'd be curious about your list. Here are a few I wonder about: motivational speakers, group facilitators, religious leaders, therapists, and—I'm coming to understand—*writers*. All the examples I can think of require a high degree of authenticity because their work is to help people see what they can't see for themselves *because it's about themselves*. Just like your job is to help students see what they can't see for themselves *about themselves*. We're not just teaching them math content—*we're helping them author their math story*.

Our effectiveness will always be limited by our ability to be authentic because children are exceptional at detecting, sniffing out, and calling out inauthenticity, and adolescents *loathe* it. When we're fake, we turn our students off. Chess players have it easy. You can become a great chess player and still be a complete jackass. Heck, you can become President of the United States and still be a complete jackass. But you know you can't even become a *mediocre* teacher unless you are constantly willing to learn about and work on yourself—continually finding ways to improve not just your Garden, *but the Tree you bring to it*. That's what separates us from Timur. Not ability or potential—simply the context of our expertise. Our exceptionalism may never look like his, but we are no less capable of expanding our potential than he is.

> Our effectiveness will always be limited by our ability to be authentic because children are exceptional at detecting, sniffing out, and calling out inauthenticity, and adolescents *loathe it*.

Let's lower the bar being placed on us and give ourselves some grace when we find ourselves measuring our effectiveness using the measures and language that the Headwinds and other Immovable

Mountains currently offer us. *Better yet, let's seize that bar and reclaim it for ourselves* and start learning how to focus on measuring the things we value as we take our journey against these unjust influences. Becoming the teachers our students need us to be requires *raising the bar on ourselves* to have a more enhanced and accurate mental model of our own Tree. It's hard to see yourself, to create the vantage—the space—to see what you need to see, especially when we're moving at the chaotic speed of school. That's why I'm trying not just to tell you what I mean by the word "vantage," but *show you why it's necessary.*

Our Trees Crave Nourishment

The Tree is a mental model of our identity that is composed of the beliefs we hold sacred about who we are as teachers of mathematics and the types of math students (and math classrooms) we are trying to create. But the Tree is more than just a catalog of our passions, values, and beliefs. *The Tree in all teachers actively seeks nourishment—craving the sense of wholeness it feels when our purpose aligns with our practice.* This idea of wholeness is found in our relationships—with ourselves, with our students, and with our colleagues on this journey—and it will be a central focus of this chapter and the next.

Note
In this chapter, the Lighthouse Reflection is in the main narrative. The Seek Vantage and Campfire Gathering can be found in Interlude 6 after this chapter.

As our emotional center, the Tree is the driver behind our actions. It's the identity that exercises agency in the Garden. Because your Tree represents the *why's* behind your teaching choices, knowledge of your Tree and how it manifests in your teaching, for *better and worse*, is essential to being able to create the vantage you need to refine your performance in the classroom. And having knowledge of each other's Trees—and having the courage to let others know ours in Campfire Gatherings and in our classrooms—is essential if we are to support each other's journey.

For Lighthouse Reflection 3, you will read five passion profiles. I'm not going to ask you to choose just one that represents you. I recognize that your passions for your work are probably too complex to fit neatly into a paragraph. The language in these profiles is intended simply to spark a conversation that creates the vantage we need to see our own uniqueness with new eyes and to help us celebrate and appreciate the uniqueness of our colleagues.

To be clear, I'm not exactly asking, Why did you become a teacher? That question was answered in Lighthouse Reflection 1 as a part of your teaching story. Nor am I asking, Why did you become a teacher of *mathematics*? I want to be inclusive of teachers on this journey who may not identify as "math teachers"—elementary and other multiple-subject teachers, specifically.

I'm explicitly asking you to think about why you *continue* to teach *right now*. What nourishes you about your work that makes you get out of bed in the morning and show up ready to tackle the expected and unexpected challenges your day inevitably will bring you? Why do you continue to pursue one of the most demanding—and perhaps one of the most underappreciated and misunderstood—careers imaginable? Through it all, what fuels your sense of sisu?

Note
While heavily adapted for the purposes of this book, language in this activity borrows from the National School Faculty Reform "Passion Profiles" protocol, which is adapted from the work "Student Profiles" by Pedro Bermudez, Belkis Cabrera, and Linda Emm. This activity stands on their shoulders.

LIGHTHOUSE REFLECTION 3: WHAT IS YOUR PASSION PROFILE?

FOCUS

As you read the Passion Profiles below, highlight or make note of language that strongly resonates with you and your reasons for why you teach. Resist the urge to attach yourself to a specific profile until you've read them all. They exist in no particular order. There are some important reflection questions to guide your thinking at the end. Because this is the fuel you will bring to the next Campfire Gathering, I invite you to be authentic with yourself about what drives you as a teacher right now.

The Gardener: A Passion for Growth

You view the individuals in your room as people first and students second. It's important to you to cultivate positive relationships with as many of your individual students as you can. You believe that knowing the unique qualities and understanding the life experiences your students bring to your class are the keys to unlocking your full potential as their teacher. You pay attention to the body language of each student in your room. If a student seems troubled, you make a deliberate point to connect with them. You are a teacher who "gets kids" and keeps current on new memes, technologies, and fads in youth culture because you want to stay relevant to their lived experiences. You recognize that many of your students have experienced or continue to experience trauma in their daily lives and create classroom environments where they can feel safe and learn how to learn. You see the value of time spent in "advisory" and "homeroom" and helping your students grow as people who strive to be their best version of themselves. A metaphor that might describe you is that of a "Gardener" who is invested in making sure all their "plants" have what they need to thrive.

When you are teaching mathematics, your passion is nourished most when you see your students developing a positive disposition about themselves as mathematical thinkers. You find flourishment most when your students have those "lightbulb moments" in your lessons that tell you they are building their math confidence and self-esteem. *Ohhh! I get it now!*

The Novelist: A Passion for Content

You want your students to love and appreciate your content as much as you do. You are interested in curriculum design, and you strive to author a yearlong learning experience for your students that consists of units of study that fit together to form a coherent story. You are bothered when a curriculum presents your content as a sequence of disjointed facts or disconnected ideas. You want your students to have a rich understanding of content and what it means to think like a mathematician (or historian, artist, scientist, etc.). You have a thorough understanding of your content area below and above your grade level, and you strive to learn more by attending conferences, reading journals, and staying current with the latest research. You embrace the opportunities to teach interdisciplinary units and enjoy thinking flexibly about content to make it more meaningful and accessible for your students. You value students' understanding of the big ideas rather than students' mastery of isolated skills. A metaphor that might describe you best is a "Novelist" who authors a coherent story arc with your teaching.

When you are teaching mathematics, you are nourished when your students see that mathematics is beautiful, useful, and coherent. You find flourishment most when your students express a love and appreciation for mathematics and become flexible thinkers who are making their own connections between mathematical ideas.

The Conductor: A Passion for the Teaching Craft

You enthusiastically embrace the inherent challenges of teaching a room filled with a diversity of learning needs. You view the collective differences in your students not as a teaching *obstacle* but as a teaching *opportunity*. Learning is dynamic and coordinated in your classroom and is evident in your lesson preparation. You carefully think about the tasks you choose and deliberately anticipate how your students will make sense of a problem and the scaffolds that will support them as they persevere in problem solving. You value productive teamwork, and students understand their roles when they're involved in group work. You have command of several different discourse strategies that students use to share their thinking with each other. You see teaching as a technical craft, and you're inspired to get better at your teaching technique so that all of your students show understanding. You're experienced at tweaking the lessons in your textbook to promote more learning for all students. A metaphor that might describe you best is that of a musical "Conductor," a maestro who crafts lessons that orchestrate productive learning opportunities for all your students.

When you are teaching mathematics, you are nourished when you see students engaged in productive struggle as they learn mathematics and share their understanding with you and others. You find flourishment most when your instructional craft provides all your students access to mathematics and growth in their understanding of it, regardless of their learning needs.

The Artist: A Passion for Curiosity and Creativity

You are passionate about student engagement, inquiry, and *play*. You want your students to love learning for learning's sake. For you, quality teaching is an artistic performance, and you can make almost anything an engaging and meaningful learning opportunity for your students. You can wear many hats as an instructor because you are a risk-taker and have no hesitations about trying something new. If you think it will help your students stay enthusiastic and engaged in learning, you're all in to give it a go! Because you're willing to fail publicly in front of your students, your students see you as a learner as well. And they are more willing to take risks of their own in class as they explore new ideas. Useful mistakes are explicitly valued in your classroom as a part of the learning process. You use storytelling as an instructional tool to make your lessons relevant and interesting to your students. Your classroom is often loud and bustling with the energy of students engaged in learning. You want your students to look forward to your class because they know it's not going to be boring—you feed off of their excitement and anticipation. You honor self-assessment, reflection, and journaling in your lessons and seek ways to make these regular classroom routines. A metaphor that might describe you best is a performance "Artist" who knows that fostering a sense of curiosity, creativity, and play is the key to a productive classroom.

When you are teaching mathematics, you are nourished when you have your students enthusiastic and engaged in their learning of mathematics. You find flourishment most when you see your students wondering, inquiring, and asking questions to you, to themselves, and to each other.

The Activist: A Passion for Social Justice

You are passionate about social justice issues in education. You're deeply bothered that some schools are better than others and that many students do not have access to quality teaching in quality schools with the necessary resources to live healthy, productive, and independent lives. For you, teaching is a political act of social justice and empowering the citizens in your classroom is your means to making this world a more just, equitable, democratic, and *human* place. You want your students to build agency and autonomy over their own learning in the classroom. You build their authority by always putting their thinking and their voice at the center of the learning process. You intentionally integrate issues of race, class, power, gender, and identity into your teaching because you want your students to develop the critical thinking skills necessary to make sense of how power operates in society. Your assessments are often not tests, but meaningful projects that invite students to synthesize new learning for themselves about how the world works. You keenly seek out your own potential biases and how your teaching practice affects the identity of your students. You are open to being called out by your students when they think you are being unfair. Power and authority are something you deliberately share with your students. You are not afraid of pushing the boundaries of what students are ready to learn and you effectively hold a safe space for difficult and uncomfortable conversations in your classrooms with your students (and perhaps in the faculty lounge with your colleagues). A metaphor that might describe you best is an "Activist" fighting for a more just world.

When you are teaching mathematics, you are nourished when you see your students making meaning for themselves, taking ownership over their own learning, and engaging in critical thinking. You find flourishment when your students are using mathematics to make sense of complex issues in the world around them.

Reflection Questions

1. Take a moment and look over the language that resonated most strongly with you in the entire activity. Imagine holding 100 pennies that you can distribute to each of the profiles. How would you distribute them in a way that reflects your passions? For example, maybe you're a teacher who puts 60 pennies on the Gardener, 30 pennies on the Novelist, and 10 on a third passion. Maybe one of these passions resonates so strongly with you that you want to put 100 pennies all on that one. Take a step back and look at your distribution. In what ways are you passionate about your work as a teacher? What nourishes you in the math classroom?

2. How do you show your passions to your students? How do your students know what inspires you and what matters most to you as a teacher? What actions do you take to let yourself be known authentically?

3. Connect your thinking back to your Teaching Story from Chapter 4. How have your passions changed over time? What might the distribution of pennies have looked like at the beginning of your career? What, if anything, caused the shift in distribution over time? How might the distribution change moving forward?

4. What might be missing in this list of passions? What language would you add?

Keep your notes. We'll use these notes as fuel for our next Campfire Gathering. ●

My Tree Actively Craves Nourishment

We all have a noble vision of equity—and we all actively nourish ourselves trying to achieve our vision of equity in our classrooms. Allow me to explain what I mean when I say that the Tree actively craves nourishment by sharing a bit about my own Tree and how it drives my decisions and actions in my Garden. I identify strongly with both the Activist and Artist passion profiles. In tandem, they define my vision of equity in the classroom and also my professional identity. Teaching predominantly juniors and seniors in Title I high schools, the Activist in me is deeply troubled by the ways mathematics serves as a gatekeeper for many students in our society. *Whatever your goals after high school, I never want mathematics to be an obstacle for you.* I say this to them verbatim almost every day. I'm motivated to create students who show me they're empowered in their life pursuits, and I create a Garden—a system of learning in my classroom—that my Tree believes positions every student as being capable mathematical thinkers regardless of the level of their academic proficiencies. That is a part of what nourishes my Tree.

But like your Tree, mine is also complex. In my day-to-day teaching life, I'm also very much an Artist in the classroom. I want to have fun! *Boredom in my classroom is my teaching nightmare.* I want my students to be engaged in mathematics that inspires them—compels them—to discuss rich, meaningful ideas that they actually want to talk about. Many times that means stepping outside of what the "standards" and my textbook say I should teach. This, too, is a part of my vision for equity in the classroom—seeing all students curious about mathematics.

Hey, Mr. O!! What you got for us today, man? When I have students who say *that* when they walk into my classroom, that is data that nourishes and validates me. I'll work my ass off for that data. Looking at standardized assessment data to see if I achieved our district-wide goal of at least a 15-point increase for 80% of my students last year? *Sorry, Boss. Not my thing. Are you going to fire me at the end of the year because of it?*

My Tree, like your Tree, drives my decisions and actions in my Garden— it informs everything from lesson planning, curriculum design, assessment, and grading, to how my classroom is set up, and so on. And the Tree in me—like the Tree in you—is always craving to be nourished by the sense of wholeness it feels when practice and purpose align, when my expertise furthers the productive math stories of my students, when they feel the empowerment and curiosity that will help them persevere through their life struggles beyond my math classroom. When I'm nourished, I feel more connected to my work, and I feel a deep, rewarding sense of efficacy in the type of relationships I am able to build with my students. I feel *alive*. These are my best days, when my flourishment is elevated.

Obviously, not every lesson has this impact. I have days—even weeks— where my nightmare is my reality: my students are listless and bored in my lessons. Despite my passion, I can't get them to engage with the content, to take risks, to ask questions and probe each other's thinking. I feel like I'm dragging them through the content—enabling their sense of helplessness rather than working to dismantle it. *Let me show you one more time how to do it. Just follow the steps, OK?* Their blank faces and disinterested body language become data points that gnaw at my Tree. I read their disengagement as their way of tacitly saying: *Nah, man. Not my thing. You gonna fail me at the end of the year because of it?*

I begin to really dread Sunday nights.

During stretches when I feel most exhausted and frustrated, I find myself disengaging and recoiling from my practice. Instead of building a sense of professional wholeness, I retreat into a life of professional dividedness. My sense of dividedness is felt in the relationships with my colleagues—even my friends notice my withdrawal. Interactions with my students become oppositional instead of collaborative as my teaching feels more like a mandate of my power rather than an invitation coming from my inner worth. Their unwavering abject apathy wears me down into a withered sense of futility and inefficacy. On my worst days, I find myself asking—sometimes with a frightening and unnerving level of emotion—*Why should I try this hard if you don't care? Why am I the hardest working person in my own classroom, right now?*

If I'm being honest, I've even said these words out loud to my students—on more than one occasion. Even without saying these words, however, I know the emotion was expressed *tacitly* countless times in my actions, my tone, my face, and the way I snap a cap on a dry-erase marker that says, *Well, I've had enough of this bullshit for today.*

As Parker Palmer says, when we teach, we project the condition of our Tree onto our students, our Gardens, and our relationships and ways of being together. I want to take a moment to return to Brenda and why I opened our journey with her math story in Chapter 1. I never taught Brenda, but her story tugs deeply at my Sea of Shame because I know that there are too many students who have left my classroom over the years thinking the same exact thing about themselves—*I am not a math person. Math isn't for me.*

This book is dedicated to my "Brendas" and my "Brendons." I want to increase the value of my mistakes with them by sharing them with you—not because they deserved a better teacher than I was able to be but because I know there were too many times when *they deserved a better teacher than I was willing to be.*

Wholeness in Our Relationships

> We cannot embrace this challenge all alone, at least, not for long: we need trustworthy relationships, tenacious communities of support, if we are to sustain the journey toward an undivided life. That journey has solitary passages, to be sure, and yet it is simply too arduous to take without the assistance of others. And because we have such a vast capacity for self-delusion, we will inevitably get lost *en route* without correctives from outside of ourselves.
>
> —Palmer, *A Hidden Wholeness* (2008, p. 10)

I appreciate you for listening and offering me some wholeness. You are a comfort, just as you are a comfort to your colleagues when you listen to them and offer them the wholeness they need. I hope you have some vantage now on what I mean when I say, *Wholeness is something we must learn to receive from others.*

Namaste. Ubuntu. Baraka. Grace. Sacred. Wholeness. These words serve to remind us that the well-being of our humanity is interrelated, interconnected. I am well only if you are well. It's a phenomenon that we can only experience together. That's one of the fundamental reasons why we create relationships in the first place: so that we can be known. But it's hard to be known when you're alone in a silo.

Nourishment comes from a sense of wholeness we feel when our purpose—the data that nourishes our Tree—aligns with our practice—our actions in our Garden. When we are nourished, we not only feel connected to our work and connected to our students, we are more willing to be open and authentic in our relationships with each other as colleagues. In these types of relationships, we don't evade our own feelings of vulnerability, choosing instead to hold space so that we can learn *from* each other and *through* each other. And we do this because we trust we won't be judged. Grace.

It's essential that we practice these types of relationships because when we lack this sense of nourishment, when we feel "unnourished," our sense of wholeness can be replaced with feelings of dividedness. And because teaching is so personal to us, our professional failures can feel *very* personal to us. It can be tempting to withdraw into the divided life because it appeals to our need to have some personal control in our chaotic professional lives. This is life in the Sea of Shame.

But we know that to find professional flourishment, we cannot retreat within ourselves and hide our failures in the silos of our classroom. The journey to flourishment requires us not just to be continually open with our hearts, centered in our passions, and connected to our work with our students—we must build the trust required to have relationships that will allow us to be open with each other as colleagues. Because we will inevitably get lost on our journey, and we will need each other to correct us on our headings. This is what we are doing at our Campfire Gatherings. We are practicing the courage to let our true, authentic, inner teacher be revealed to each other so that we may learn through each other's lived experience.

KEY TAKEAWAYS FROM CHAPTER 6

* It's hard to create vantage on yourself—especially when you're moving at the speed of school.

* Effective teaching requires authenticity. Our effectiveness will always be limited by our ability to be authentic with our students and with each other. When we're fake, we turn others off.

* We all crave nourishment. What that nourishment looks like, is personal to each of us, because we all carry a unique passion profile.

* A nourishing sense of wholeness can be found in our relationships—if we learn to receive it from others.

INTERLUDE 6:
HOW DO YOUR STUDENTS SEE YOU?

SEEK VANTAGE 3: NEW EYES ON YOUR TREE

VANTAGE

To frame this Seek Vantage, I offer you this window from my teaching story so you can know a bit more about me and my journey as an imperfect and unfinished math teacher. I also offer it as an example of how we, as colleagues, can position each other as active partners in each other's professional learning by helping each other see what we cannot see for ourselves.

First Period Gut Punch

It was sometime during late September, about the fifth week of school, when I plopped down, defeated, on Dr. P's couch in his office. We hadn't known each other that long, but I had sought guidance from him before because he had built so much relationship capital with the students and their parents over the years as the Assistant Principal. He was also Latino and understood the lived experiences of our students in ways that I did not. I trusted his vantage and valued his guidance.

I was in my seventh year of teaching, but my first at this school, a Title I high school in a predominantly working- and middle-class Latinx community located in the South Bay of Los Angeles County. It was my first year teaching within a public school system. Most of my classes weren't going that well, but they were productive enough that I was able to gain traction and build some positive culture with my students.

First period was a different story, however. It was a section of 38 high school seniors in Algebra 2 who, as ninth graders, had had four different Algebra 1 teachers. Three of those teachers had quit during that year. All of these 38 seniors had failed a math class at some point in their high school career. I called it my "First Period Gut Punch." Every day, I'd show up to work, get emotionally punched in the gut by my own inefficacy, and then have to carry on with my teaching day from there.

This was foreign territory for me. I had tried everything in my toolkit. Nothing worked. I remember feeling that if I could get 20% of the students to do math 20% of the time, that was a win. The culture was hostile. I had no influence, no rapport, and no productive relationships with them. My only means of maintaining order was to use my power—*my voice*—in my role as a teacher over them. *If you don't pay attention, there will be consequences ...* Even though I knew they knew I knew there would, in fact, be no consequences. None that really mattered to them anyway. This was a reality they had grown accustomed to in the math classroom. I was just another adult at the front of the room trying to tell them to learn something they weren't interested in learning—just another human in the machinery of a math education system that had diminished their mathematical identities to the point that many resented math class.

My expertise was so outmatched by my position that 8:55 a.m. on Friday mornings, the end of first period, was the most relieved I felt at any moment during the week—or weekend. *Well, at least I don't have to do that again for 71 hours and 5 minutes.*

I began to think of those ninth grade teachers who had quit. I didn't want to quit, but I didn't know how much longer I could keep going like this.

What am I doing wrong, Dr. P? Seriously, I don't know what else I can do.

He inhaled slowly. And then he gave me one of the most useful nuggets of wisdom I've ever received in my career:

Chase, it's important that you know how your students see you.

In the next few days, I invite you to spend time in each other's classrooms thinking about how your students perceive you. How would they describe you as a math teacher? What would they say you value most in math class?

Here are some questions to think about before, during, and after the observations to help focus your thinking.

Before the observation(s): Reflect on your own Tree and the language you highlighted in the Passion Profiles.

- What do you value most when it comes to student learning in your math classroom?

- How do these values show themselves in your teaching? How are they expressed in your classroom norms?

- Imagine being one of your students in your classroom. How do they know what you're passionate about? Looking at your actions, how would they describe the classroom that nourishes your Tree?

During the observation(s): Look/Listen/Feel

- What is being valued in the math classroom? What do students spend time doing? What do they seem to value at the moment?

- Who's talking in the classroom? Who's asking questions? And what is being said?

- What classroom norms do you notice? How are these norms communicated to students? How are they enforced?

At the end of observation(s): Engage in 2 minutes of relationship building. See prompts in Seek Vantage 1 in Interlude 4.

After the observation(s): Before continuing on your journey, take a pause and reflect on your experience.

- What have you learned about your values and your passions that you may not have realized before? What might you add to the Lighthouse Reflection from the beginning of Chapter 6?

- What new eyes did you gain about your Tree when you visited other classrooms? How do you show your students what you value as a teacher?

- How might that new learning affect your teaching practice? What might you be considering doing differently? How might your Tree need to be pruned? ●

CAMPFIRE GATHERING AGENDA 3: SHARE YOUR PASSION PROFILES

RELATIONSHIPS

Purpose: To appreciate the unique passion(s) you bring to the classroom.

At this gathering, you'll each have about 5-7 minutes of uninterrupted time to share your reasons why you teach and the passion(s) you bring to your classrooms. To prepare, look at your notes from "Lighthouse Reflection 3: What is your passion profile?"

What do you want to share with the group about your teaching passion(s)? What do you want them to know about your Tree and the authentic, emotional teacher within you? ●

NOTES

_____

_____

_____

_____

_____

_____

_____

_____

_____

_____

_____

_____

_____

_____

_____

_____

_____

THE STEEP PRICE OF A DIVIDED LIFE

Where We've Been

In Part 2 of our journey, we have been taking actions to build our culture of professionalism as we've shared our stories and looked through windows together. We're learning how to create vantage for ourselves and for each other so we can bring to the surface our beliefs about our professional identity and our vision of equity. We cannot test a belief we do not yet see.

Where We're Going

In Chapter 7, we will bring closure to this part of our journey by returning to and continuing the Rudy Story from the Introduction. We will look through the window together to describe the fundamental shifts that we will be making and actions we will be taking in Part 3.

I pay a steep price when I live a divided life-feeling fraudulent, anxious about being found out, and depressed by my dividedness. How can I affirm another's identity when I deny my own? How can I trust another's integrity when I defy my own? A fault line runs down the middle of my life, and whenever it cracks open-divorcing my words and actions from the truth I hold within-things around me get shaky and start to fall apart.

—Palmer, *Hidden Wholeness* (2004, p. 5)

A Moment of Vantage That Split My Biased Tree in Two

I'll be talking about my Tree again in this chapter. The stories I share are from the rawest, most visceral moment of my teaching career when I felt most divided between my identity as a teacher and my actions in my Garden. As you read, I ask that you give me the same grace you gave Lillian (and the grace that I hope you are learning to give to each other). My flourishment was at an all-time low—anger, hurt, and bitterness are the emotions that consumed me at the time.

The events I am about to describe happened during my ninth year of teaching, almost three years after the First Period Gut Punch story (from Interlude 6) when Dr. P told me, *Chase, it's important to know how your students see you.* Rudy represented a major turning point in my teaching story—a turning point that eventually led me to you, this book, and our journey together.

Before continuing forward, I ask that you *please reread the Rudy Story* from the Introduction and revisit your answers to the questions at the end of the story. Your thinking is most likely different now than it was when you first read it. You may have new eyes and may see new things that were tacit to you before.

What the Hell Are You Doing, Chase?

What did I do with Rudy, at 7:00 p.m., less than 48 hours before his potential graduation ceremony and earning his diploma—his cap and gown hanging in his bedroom closet?

I have to fail you, Rudy.

His face fell. He knew it too. Then he mustered his famous Rudy smile one more time, looked me in the eye, and gave me a genuine thank you as he shook my hand. *Whomp, whomp, whomp.* Heavy went Rudy's steps down the metal ramp from my bungalow classroom. And that was that.

I flopped in my chair. I covered my face. And I wept into the palms of my hands. *What the hell are you doing, Chase?*

Stunned, despondent, sisu-less, I began to stare blankly at my classroom space. I had started to pack up my room earlier in the day, and now it was in that weird in-between space. If you've ever moved out of an apartment you've loved, you know the feeling. It's that

Continued →

→ Continued

moment when you haven't left yet, but the space no longer feels like your home.

Looking through teary eyes and in my emotional wake, I saw my classroom as a system of learning in a way that I could see—from a vantage point I had never had before—that revealed to me how divorced my purpose and my practice truly were. This giant fault line emerged down the middle of my Tree. It had always been there— tacitly. I had sensed it before, but now I could not deny it because it was split wide open. My Tree was cleaved in two, down to its roots. Everything seemed so pointless.

It started with that deep internal voice whose authority was beyond reproach. Looking back now, I know it was my Future Tree. *What the hell are you doing, Chase? What story are you making here for yourself? What story are you making for your students? Look at yourself—this isn't who we are. You're wrong about something, and you don't see it yet. And it's time you figured it out.*

Whomp, whomp, whomp. It's Rudy. And he's back in my classroom doorway just 20 minutes after he had left. *Hey Mr. Orton. I just talked to Dr. P, and he said he won't be able to finalize the grades until noon tomorrow. And I can have an extension, if you're willing to offer it. He says you don't have to. And I get it Mr. O, I'm the one who put myself in this position. I don't deserve another chance.*

I took a deep breath, taking in and appreciating how very different our lived experiences had been since our last moment together. Looking back, I wonder how he saw me in that moment in my puffy-eyed, sisu- less state. *Jeez . . . is this what teaching does to people?*

I told Rudy to come back in the morning. I needed some time to think. I already knew what I was going to do before the last *whomp*. What I needed was to figure out *why*.

Rudy showed up the next morning. He worked on problems on the whiteboard for a few more hours while I gave him feedback and finished cleaning up my classroom. When I was done, I told him he was done. He looked a bit confused. *You've passed, Rudy. You're graduating.*

He began to speak. I cut him off. *Look, Rudy, it's time to go do more meaningful things with your life than this bullshit. We're both finished here. I'm proud of you. Now go.*

A short while after he left, I locked my classroom door. *Whomp, whomp, whomp.* My own steps sounded heavier than Rudy's ever did. That voice was still following me, quieter now, but no less troubling— *What the hell are you doing, Chase?*

Looking Through the Window: The Steep Price of a Divided Life

Every summer since I was 12, I've spent long days on my father's farm in Oregon sitting on a tractor harvesting hay. The tractor seat has been a setting for long moments of mulling over the course of my career. At the end of each school year, it was the mundane type of boredom I needed to get some vantage on everything that had happened—all the *data*. It was an unbounded, free-form time to think without having to take action—a time to compile and compress all my learning and to find ways to improve my craft. Just going around different hay fields in a tractor seat. Usually not much faster than walking speed. Right turn. Keep the tractor straight. Right turn. Keep it straight, right turn . . . for hours, for days, for weeks.

There was a lot to think about the summer after Rudy graduated. I mulled over that moment of vantage for *fields* of right turns, grappling with this deep sense of conflict within myself. *How do I describe this overwhelming sense of dividedness I feel as a teacher?* As a window into my own internal debate at the time, let me share how my thoughts evolved around the fields that summer, right turn by right turn, as I mulled over the events with Rudy.

A Summer of Right Turns

It was Rudy's words that stuck in my craw the most: *I'm the one that put myself in this position—I don't deserve another chance.* Position. Deserve. Now those are interesting words, Rudy. Let's talk about your *position* and what you *deserve*. Who *positioned* you here? Right turn.

You're right Rudy. You put yourself in that position. And I'm disappointed you put me—*put us*—in that position. I worked hard for you, Rudy. You waited until the last minute. Our relationship *deserved* better. I *deserved* better. *Why did you do this to me?* Right turn.

And Dr. P! He literally just sent you *back* to this position. So did you *really* put yourself here the second time? *What the hell was Dr. P thinking anyway, putting me in that position? I didn't deserve that.* Right turn.

> You know Rudy isn't the source of your troubles, Chase. It's unproductive to be mad at him. Or mad at Dr. P. *Stop blaming them.* Right turn.

Continued →

→ Continued

Look, Rudy knew my *system*. We had talked about it for months. He knew the rules—the conditions I had refined over the years to ensure any student could pass. Extra help every day after school. Unlimited retakes on exams. Homework was optional. All he had to do was show me he could do the core problems on the exams and complete his projects. Aren't there supposed to be consequences for waiting until the last moment? Right turn.

So why did you pass him? Right turn.

So why did you pass him? Right turn.

So why did you pass him, Chase?

Because that's what I felt Rudy *deserved, alright?! It's what he was owed from the broken system that put him there.* Besides, he was *ready enough* for what was next. What lesson was he going to learn by me giving him an F? What good would have come of it? Right turn.

What good came from all the Fs you gave to the others, Chase? Did those students learn the lessons you wanted them to? Were you *feeling* your purpose when you decided what they were owed by this *unjust system?* Right turn. Keep it straight. Right turn.

See it from their perspective. What would they say to you now? Did they feel like you rooted for them? Did they feel like you saw their brilliance like you saw Rudy's? Or did they feel seen mostly for their *deficits* because that's what you saw in them most? Right turn. Keep it straight. Right turn.

Own it, Chase. You can only reflect back the brilliance you're capable of seeing in them. And you're biased about the brilliance you see—and the brilliance you don't. Your students know it. *They feel your bias.* Right turn. Keep it straight. Right turn.

And you're trying to excuse yourself by saying you've created this equitable system in your classroom. And now you're aware that it's a crock of bullshit because it's only as equitable as your behavior and your actions—your *expertise*—can effectively *show* your students that you believe in them. And some of your students don't feel like you believe in them, Chase. You may not say it to them with your words, but you know they are watching.

Despite your best efforts for 9 years, Chase, math class still isn't working for some of your students *because of you.*

Right turn. Right turn. Right turn. Right turn . . .

> *Do we all feel this way at some point as teachers?* I can't go into next school year feeling like this about my teaching. Something better needs to come from this experience than bitterness and dividedness . . . Right turn.
>
> > *Position. Deserved.* Time to put it together, Chase. You've run out of hay fields.

What Would We Say If We Were All Positioned in the Room Together?

PRACTICE MIRROROING: SOMETHING I HEAR YOU SAYING IS . . .

RELATIONSHIPS

If we were gathered at a Campfire Gathering at the beginning of the school year after that summer, the following section is what I would say during a Mirroring Conversation because I would want to hear you speak, not necessarily my own words, but the meaning and the significance you hear beneath my words. I would need your help creating vantage that I can't do alone.

As you read ahead, imagine us sitting in a room together and I'm telling you this not long after the Rudy Story occurred. Hear me as if I am one of your colleagues. What do you hear beneath my words? What would you reflect back to me? How might your reflection of me help enhance my identity by helping me understand myself more fully?

Try it out with: *Something I hear you saying is _____.*

There are no right answers. I'm not fishing for anything. These are all earnest questions to expand your capacity to paraphrase and mirror each other. *It's an essential skill in our relationships to create vantage with each other.* ●

The Fall Term After Rudy

I've thought a lot about Rudy lately and what I've learned from my dilemma with him since last June. The thing I was most frustrated about that moment was that it was *private*—just me and Rudy. If I had a wish, I wanted all of Rudy's former teachers and administrators in the room with me so that they could see the interconnectedness of our work and say to them—without blaming them:

> This is the Rudy we produced. He is the result of 12 years of our best efforts. What burden of the responsibility do we all share in Rudy's position? None of us wanted this. Rudy deserved better. And so do our Rudys now. How do we do better, together? Because I know my best, alone, isn't good enough for some of my students. We need to be learning from this moment. What do you see? And how do you see it?

And I started wondering, what would we say to each other? As colleagues all bonded together by Rudy's lived experience and his charming smile, together for the first time, would we agree on whether or not Rudy should graduate? Would we realize how the silos of our classroom prevent us from seeing that we are all building the same connected math story for each of our students?

In that tractor seat, I realized that I wanted us all to see that when we work in a system that explicitly encourages us and tacitly conditions us to talk about our students as if they were a test score that needed to be raised, we are no longer able to talk with each about the things that really matter to us math teachers. I didn't become a teacher because I wanted to train test takers—none of us did. I wanted my students to love mathematics and to believe that they can be successful at it. What do you value most? And what conversations do we need to have so we can start measuring the things we value with each other?

I'm also deeply angry at an education system that positions me in a way that I have to decide what a student deserves after they've sat through over 10 years of math classes where their learning needs weren't met.

Here are my two options when it comes to this year's seniors in my Algebra 2 classes who don't "show mastery" by June 8 at 7:00 p.m.:

- Option A: Advocate for them by furthering them along their path to more productive things than Algebra 2. They'll most likely have to take remedial math classes depending on where they go to college. And I'll worry for them, but at least they'll be in a position to make a new story for themselves.

- Option B: Give them an "F" and defend what we already know to be an oppressive and unjust math education system that says that fluency in Algebra 2 is a worthwhile pursuit and an essential component of being "career and college ready." I can take cover behind my professional mandates when it comes to "academic credit" and say these "Fs" accurately reflect the grade they deserve. I could keep telling myself: *It's my job. I can't just pass kids. It wouldn't be fair to the students I've failed before.*

Here's what I realized over the summer: it's *already too late* to be fair to those former students of mine. The harm has been done. What about our students right now? What are they owed—what is fair to them in their position?

I'm choosing Option A because I can't help but feel that the grades I dole out are not truly a measure of what my students know so much as they are a reflection of all our collective efforts working within an inequitable system. *It's not our fault.* I don't blame any of us. At every grade level in the math education system, we are given a net and asked to catch water to fill their buckets. It tears me apart having to measure a *human being* by how much water we've been able to catch with our nets after all those years. It's not fair to any of us—and it's dehumanizing. When we diminish the identity of our students, we diminish ourselves.

Even if I had a bucket to catch water to fill their buckets, so much of the whole enterprise—not teaching mathematics to the young—but the system of math education itself—the water, the bucket, the whole damn act . . . it all feels so pointless to me right now. I no longer want to work in a system that positions me in front of a locked gate with the key in my pocket deciding who deserves access and who doesn't. *Who the hell am I to decide what a kid deserves?*

Here's what I learned about what my students deserve: *they deserve more of my grace.* Beyond that, my work should always focus on what students *need.*

(Big sigh.)

I also want to share something else. I've been thinking a lot about my own actions in the classroom. I realize that after 9 years of teaching, I still have some personal growth to do, especially when it comes to my behavior when I'm frustrated with my students. I'm aware that I have tacit biases that reveal themselves in my choices as I create and implement a system of learning in my classroom. I acknowledge that I do things that communicate to students that I'm rooting for some more than others. I *tell* my students I believe they're capable—but I'm aware that I don't *show* that to them all the time. It'd be a great help if y'all could pop into my classes every now and again to collect some data and give me feedback.

Continued →

→ Continued

> - What might be some behaviors or actions that tell some of my students that I don't believe they're capable?
>
> - What am I doing that might be turning some of my students off?
>
> - *Who's my math class not working for and why?*
>
> I know it may seem weird at first, but I need your help seeing what I cannot see for myself. And I'd like to see it sooner. Will you help me?

Looking Through the Window: It's Not What You Tell Them, It's What You Show Them

The United States is always reforming but not always improving. The most alarming aspect of classroom teaching in the United States is not how we are teaching now, but that we have no mechanism for getting better . . . Although *teachers hold the key* they teach in a system that currently works against improvement.

—Stigler and Hiebert, *The Teaching Gap* (2009, pp. xviii-xix, emphasis mine)

It's not what you tell them, it's what you show them will be a frequent mantra in the chapters to come. As we've discussed, stories are one of my ways of sharing authority with you. They position you to make your own meaning of the windows we look through together—because the most important meaning of all is *yours*. In addition to sharing authority with you, stories are my way of *showing* you, rather than simply *telling* you, what I've learned, seen, and heard over the course of my career.

From a certain vantage, the Rudy Story could be about a high school teacher who's blaming teachers "beneath him." *What are those elementary teachers teaching these days? My students can't even do basic mathematics! And this is what the middle school is offering us? These kids aren't mature enough to learn in a high school classroom? My goodness. How can I possibly do my job if they're all so inept at theirs?*

I know this unproductive, hierarchical version of the blame game is, unfortunately, quite prevalent in some corners of our professional landscape. I trust that I've earned enough credibility by now that you know that I'm not blaming anyone within the system. I wanted us all in the room together so we could see how intimately interconnected our work really is—colleagues who all care about the well-being of the young people we inherit and pass along to each other. The Rudy Story is my way of showing you that we are all engaged in the same task—helping each of our students author a math story that is empowering and *unfinished*.

> The Rudy Story is my way of showing you that we are all engaged in the same task-helping each of our students author a math story that is empowering and unfinished.

I can't just tell you we need to start leaving our silos—I have to show you *why we must*. I'm extending *an urgent plea* for us to leave our silos so that we can rise up against a system that, despite our best individual efforts, actively diminishes the math identities of our students and erodes their sense of mathematical agency. The system of math education is not only destroying our cultural relationship with mathematics but also destroying the vitality of our profession by continually eroding our professional flourishment, individually and collectively.

We hold the key—and it's the key to our own silos. And we must use them because *there is no closure to the Rudy Story—it continues today, right now*. We must challenge the Headwinds and abandon the current culture of isolationism that diminishes our professional identities as teachers, replacing it with a new culture of professionalism—as defined by the Beacons—where we learn how to become active partners in each other's learning.

> We hold the key-and it's the key to our own silos. And we must use them because there is no closure to the Rudy Story-it continues today, right now.

Once we start to step out of our silos, we innately begin to build the relationships we need to help each other further our teaching craft. My hope is that by this point in our journey, you are talking more authentically with each other—more honestly—about what is going well in your classroom and what isn't. As you do, I hope you're offering each other grace as you become compassionate, active partners in each other's learning. Grace is what it takes to be an imperfect and unfinished math teacher continually practicing the Art of Not Knowing.

We Are Stewards of Our Cultural Math Story

Most of what I share in this book, I learned in my career after Rudy graduated.

In the years before Rudy, I had measured myself as a teacher based on my ability to design a fair system of learning where any student, regardless of their prior academic performance, could pass. I would tell my students, *If you show up and work hard, you will be successful at the mathematics I'm teaching you.* After years of continually refining my system, this damaging, tacit belief had formed: *I have given my students all they need for success. If students fail, that's on them—not me. If they can't learn in this system, then they don't deserve to pass.* It sounds so terrible to write those words all these years later. I was doing the same thing as that "crappy teacher" in college—I was blaming my students for their failure to thrive because I assumed I had given them everything they needed.

That single realization gave me new eyes on my own professional identity. I realized how conditioned I had become—and how conditioned our students had become—to see "math class" as an exchange of commodities. *If I give my teacher what they need and act like a good student, they will give me a good grade.* This exchange defined my relationship with my students as one of authority and dominance *over them*. Sharing authority fully with my students in this dynamic would always be impossible. So long as they saw me as a judge who must be appeased and pleased, I was never going to be in a position to have an equitable relationship with my students—individually or collectively.

In the years that followed Rudy, I began to see myself less as a teacher of mathematical content and more as someone helping young people author an empowered math story. As I did, my classroom became less "content-focused" and more "story-focused." Once I made this shift, I was able to share authority in my classroom in ways that I could never do before. I could spend more time relating with my students in ways that weren't about mastery of content, but on authoring their math story. Instead of creating an equitable system that focused on gaps in "academic performance," I spent time creating an equitable system that focused on changing and empowering "math stories." It allowed me to hone in on what really motivated me—the same thing that motivates all of us—enhancing the mathematical identity and fostering the agency of the students we serve.

> *Instead of creating an equitable system that focused on gaps in "academic performance," I spent time creating an equitable system that focused on changing and empowering "math stories."*

By no means was I a perfect teacher. I was still *very much imperfect*, but I was much more *fulfilled* as a teacher because my problems of practice became more explicitly about my students' math identity and their sense of agency. It was as if it took the first nine years of teaching to finally get to the point when the real teacher in me began showing up. *Why did I spend so much time doing that when I could've been doing this?*

I am asking you to make the same shift in your professional identity as well and invite you to think *less* of yourself as a teacher of mathematical content and *more* of yourself as a steward of our cultural math story. When we make this shift, we begin to pave a pathway for us to create the types of math classes that will work for more of our students and can begin to rehabilitate our cultural math story. Throughout Part 3, we will explore the actions we can take to create a "story-focused" Garden—a math class where students are more likely to author an empowering math story that remains unfinished. We will also explore why we gain more professional flourishment for ourselves when we make the shift to a "story-focused" Garden.

KEY TAKEAWAYS FROM CHAPTER 7

* For several chapters, we've talked about how hard it is—but how essential it is—to seek vantage on our own beliefs and actions. In this chapter, I offered myself and the Rudy Story as a window for you to model what I mean by this.

* The Rudy Story is also my way of showing you that we are all engaged in the same task. As stewards of our cultural math story, we are helping each of our students author a math story that is empowering and *unfinished*. We must leave our silos so that we can rise up against a system that, despite our best individual efforts, actively diminishes the math identities of our students and erodes their sense of mathematical agency.

* The current system of math education is not only destroying our cultural relationship with mathematics but also destroying the vitality of our profession by continually eroding our professional flourishment, individually and collectively. We must challenge the Headwinds and abandon the current culture of isolationism that diminishes our professional identities as teachers, replacing it with a new culture of professionalism—as defined by the Beacons—where we learn how to become active partners in each other's learning.

* We hold the key—and it's the key to our own silos. And we must use them because *there is no closure to the Rudy Story—it continues today, right now.*

INTERLUDE 7:
WHY IS MATH CLASS NOT WORKING FOR SOME STUDENTS?

In your professional library, which books are the most worn, the most beloved? Which ones do you find yourself returning to when you need to lift up your teaching spirits or go to for inspiration? I'd be curious about your list. I want to tell you about one on my list.

My mother has always had a knack for knowing the perfect book to get me at the perfect time. As I started my teaching journey, she offered me a copy of *Courage to Teach* by Parker Palmer. *You're going to need this book someday, son.* In the middle of my second year of teaching, that "someday" had arrived. Remember that naive 22-year-old college kid who said, *How hard can math teaching be?* He had become a discouraged 24-year-old teacher who, just barely into his second year of teaching, was already doubting his teaching chops and wondering if it was time to go back to grad school. *I'm not the math teacher I'd thought I'd be by now.*

By a twist of fate, Parker Palmer happened to be giving a one-day workshop on a Saturday at a nearby school. I had just started to read *Courage to Teach*, and his message resonated so strongly with me that I felt compelled to go. *My teaching soul needs this right now.*

In the workshop, we did a similar "best day/worst day" writing exercise that I am inviting you to do for Lighthouse Reflection 4. I didn't know anyone at the workshop—everyone was a stranger to me in my small group. As we shared, I had this profound realization: *I'm not alone. We are all struggling to find wholeness in our work as teachers.*

While that offered me a bit of comfort, as the end of the day approached, I still felt a nagging sense of imposter syndrome. During a break in the afternoon, I mustered my courage to walk up to Parker to say thank you and share what I had been feeling as a result of being in the workshop. It was the only time we've ever talked. I don't quite remember the exchange—the words that we said—but I remember the feeling he offered me. It was the thing we all need as imperfect teachers when we are struggling to find the courage to remain unfinished—*grace.*

I want to thank Parker Palmer for that moment. And I invite you to reach out to your own mentors and colleagues who have shown you grace in your career. More important, I would like us to see how empowering it can be to give grace to others. We never know when we're the "Parker Palmer" to another teacher. We are all learning through each other. And we have the power to offer each other the grace we need to find wholeness in our imperfection and the courage to stay unfinished.

In Chapter 6, I talked a bit about how I feel and act on my "best" days when my Tree is feeling nourished—and also on my "worst" days when I feel overwhelmed and discouraged by the Dump in my Garden. Looking through this window, you had a chance to see how my Artist/Activist Tree is present in both of these moments as I crave the nourishment of seeing my students engaged, curious, and empowered.

In this Lighthouse Reflection, you will engage in some thinking about your "best" and your "worst" days as a teacher. When we look at those contrasting moments at the same time, we can see how our Tree is equally present in both moments. During our best days, our Trees are awash in nourishment. And during our worst, our Trees are suffering from a lack of wholeness. We see this in my successes and failures to engage and empower students in the math classroom. We saw this with Lillian too as she tries and fails to make sure all of her students have a grasp of the basics and a foundation of fluency for her sixth grade students.

LIGHTHOUSE REFLECTION 4: YOUR BESTS AND WORSTS

FOCUS

The Tree is our emotional center that is always craving nourishment. Take a moment to think about when you felt most nourished and "unnourished" by your work in the classroom. Perhaps it was a conversation with a math student or a whole class, a particular math lesson or a unit of study that lasted several weeks.

1. Fill up one side of a sheet of paper jotting down your "best moments" as a teacher of mathematics. These are the moments that make you smile about yourself still. And perhaps memories that you will have for the rest of your career.

2. Now flip the sheet of paper and fill up the other side writing about one of your "worst days" as a teacher of mathematics. These may be moments when you wanted to quit.

3. Read what you wrote about your best days and ask yourself the following:

   - Why are these moments so nourishing for me? How is my purpose aligned with my practice in these moments?

   - What is the data that I value most in these moments that is signaling to me that I am successfully achieving my vision of equity?

   - What emotions do I feel when I'm nourished?

   - In what ways does my wholeness affect my relationships with students?

Read what you wrote about your worst days and ask yourself:

- Why are these moments so "unnourishing" for me?

- What is the data that I'm collecting that is telling me that my expertise is falling short of achieving my vision of equity?

- What emotions do I feel when I feel divided, discouraged, or disheartened?

- In what ways does my dividedness affect my relationships with students?

4. Now take in both sides of the sheet of paper at once. Remember, your Tree is your emotional center that is always craving nourishment.

- What nourishes your Tree?

- What does it look like when you're achieving equity? What emotions do you feel? What actions do you take?

- What does it look like when you're *not* achieving equity? What emotions do you feel? What actions do you take?

- How might your emotions be getting in your own way? ●

Math class isn't working for some of your students. You already have some beliefs about why, and you already have a history of taking actions to address their learning needs. You have a *story* you are telling yourself about these students. In this Seek Vantage, I invite you to shift your perspective on these students by creating some vantage so you can test your beliefs about why some of your students are struggling and question some of your actions as you go about meeting their needs.

SEEK VANTAGE 4: NEW EYES ON YOUR DUMP

VANTAGE

Here are some questions to think about before, during, and after the observations to help focus your thinking.

Before the observation(s): Reflect on your own Dump.

- Who's math class not working for and why?

- What is the data you see from these students that tells you they are not authoring a productive math story?

- What assumptions or beliefs have you formed about their behavior and what they need? What stories do you make about this data?

During the observation(s): Look/Listen/Feel. To the best of your ability, observe students for whom math class is not working. Watch without detachment and try to live their experience in the classroom.

- What data do these students produce? How do they exercise their math identity?
- Why do they act this way? What story might they be telling themselves?
- What would those students need to see to change the story they are telling themselves?

At the end of observation(s): Engage in 2 minutes of relationship building. See prompts in Seek Vantage 1 in Interlude 4.

After the observation(s): Before continuing on your journey, take a pause and reflect on your experience.

- What have you learned about your own students? Why is math class not working for them?
- What new eyes do you have on your own beliefs about what these students need? What unproductive beliefs might you want to test?
- What new eyes do you have on your own actions? What unproductive actions might you want to question?

CAMPFIRE GATHERING AGENDA 4: SHARE YOUR BESTS AND WORSTS

RELATIONSHIPS

Purpose: To celebrate your learning together and to further your practice of giving grace to each other.

At this gathering, you'll each have about 5-7 minutes of uninterrupted time to talk more deeply about what nourishes your Tree—and how you feel on your worst days. To prepare, look at your notes from "Lighthouse Reflection 4: Your Bests and Worsts."

What do you want to share with the group about what you wrote? What would you like to reveal? What experiences would you like to hear reflected back at you?

PART 3

CHANGING OUR CULTURAL MATH STORY

A WINDOW INTO A STORY-FOCUSED MATH CLASS

Where We've Been

Parts 1 and 2 have been about discovery and reflection as we fostered our new culture of professionalism and learned to reflect, calibrate, and collaborate as active partners in each other's professional growth. Too often in our professional development, we are forced to talk about our math teaching without first having an opportunity to talk about and *appreciate* the lived experiences that make us unique not just as math teachers but as people. That's why we've invested a significant amount of time and pages understanding and exploring our own internal landscapes as math teachers and what nourishes us.

Where We're Going

In Part 3, we will explore the actions we can take to create a "story-focused" Garden—a math class in which not only can you find more professional flourishment but where students are more likely to begin authoring their own empowering math story as well. Chapter 8 serves as a giant window for exploring these actions. Here, I will draw together all the things we have talked about into one story—the Headwinds and the Beacons, the Tree and the passions teachers bring to their classrooms, the Garden as a story-making machine where math stories are authored, and how hard it is to cultivate a story-focused Garden when an Island of Practice is dominated by the Headwinds. We will look through this window throughout the chapters and interludes in Part 3 to frame the equity actions that keep the math stories of our students thriving and empower us to change our cultural relationship with mathematics.

So long as a single poem of yours remains somewhere,
     even on the wind,
so long as you have been sincere,
even if only the sparrow has taken notice,
     you will be realized,
even if only to one young mind,
your wills, prophecies and odes to be fulfilled,
and will quench the ravaging thirst of
     some young heart,
words
     are
          worlds . . .

-Ozzy Klate
(February 25, 1977 – December 15, 1994),
excerpt from "In Nature, As Nature"
(1995, pp. 43-44)

Setting the Stage for Part 3

The Headwinds and the Beacons—my language for them and how I came to form them—are the result of several years of work in a district that I call Headwinds Unified School District, or simply, The District. During my time there, I had the unique vantage of working with teachers in K-12 classrooms in a way that allowed me to put the whole "story" together. It was here that I learned to refine and calibrate "lesson study" into a teacher-centered, teacher-directed process that you see here in this book.

➤ Let's build some culture—some relationship with each other—by talking about who we are as teachers and develop a shared appreciation of our unique visions of equity.

➤ Let's spend time in each other's classrooms seeking vantage from the students' perspective so we can better test our beliefs and question our actions.

> Let's engage in purposeful, deliberate conversations with each other as we reflect on our beliefs, calibrate our actions, and collaborate as active partners in each other's professional learning.

> Throughout the process, let's remember "sisu" and give each other the grace we need as we sustain each other's flourishment in the Headwinds.

The professionals in The District were all good people—principals, teachers, staff, and district administrators. They all wanted their students to be successful in math class. But as a system, they tightly held on to the Headwinds and to the belief that a content-focused, data-driven, assess-weekly approach was the most productive way to teach mathematics. It was a challenging place to work for the teachers who believed a story-centered Garden was the most productive way to help students develop a positive relationship with mathematics.

To be very clear, I'm *deeply indebted* to all of the people in The District for the opportunity to work there—even the "District Chief of Data," who we will meet near the end of this chapter. If I sound harsh, I am harsh on the system that incentivized many of these caring professionals to adopt a philosophical approach to teaching mathematics that is not only unproductive but also fundamentally misguided—a net designed for catching water.

Headwinds Unified School District

The District ran a top-down system of management—a single district office managed several elementary schools, a middle school, and a high school. All in all, it wasn't a bad place to be—unless, that is, you cared about the health and well-being of our cultural math story and about the mathematical identities of these students.

Principals, depending on their motivations, mitigated the damaging impact of The District—at their own professional peril. *Do what you feel is best for your math students. I will take the heat.* And they did. Some were "reassigned" or "pushed out." Others focused on making sure they—and their teachers—were compliant in using the adopted curriculum, pacing plans, and common assessments. *These are the things that the district office says we need to do. Therefore, these are things that I need you to do. So go tell your students what they need to do—get more right answers on tests!* If principals did this well enough, they were rewarded as a "Distinguished School" and some even earned a promotion to The District Office.

Raising test scores seemed to be the only goal The District seemed to talk about when it came to professional development, curriculum, and pedagogy, and it was pervasive in their language as they talked about their "low kids" and their "high fliers." Many teachers embraced this approach. Some tolerated it. A few actively rebuffed it. None seem nourished by it.

The middle and high school math classrooms seemed to be particularly distressing. By then, student math stories had become so damaged that the "content-focused Garden" wasn't working for the teachers. But they had no other options. They were stuck, lost in the Fog of Better. The younger teachers sensed the need to connect with students—to repair some of the damage done to them. But they were outmatched by the scale of the task of teaching 150 students each day who, frankly, no longer gave a damn about "math class." I had a First Period Gut Punch—these teachers had multiple versions of their own gut punch periods. They were doing their best just to survive.

Physical silos were everywhere. And the hierarchical blame game was being played as each teacher blamed the teacher before them for not preparing their students better. High school teachers looked down on the middle school teachers who looked down on the elementary teachers. Somewhere, I imagine, is a college math professor looking down on these high school teachers. *What is going on down there? Why don't my students know their content?*

Rankings between the elementary schools—based on test scores—became a part of their lexicon. A culture of isolationism was prevalent. Physical silos became emotional silos. Within schools, some teachers felt blamed for being "the weak link." Some claimed that they had been "put on notice" because of their low student test scores. Not surprisingly, most teachers were extremely nervous teaching in front of each other. *What will they think of my teaching? What if a student asks me a question I can't answer? Will they judge me?* The Sea of Shame was a powerful influence on their professional landscape.

With the Headwinds this strong, many teachers clung *hard* to their turf and guarded it as if there wasn't enough turf to go around. Ideas did not flow freely. Resources were not shared. Minds were never changing. Ears were really small. Everyone was hunkered down in their camps. On one side, you had the "old guard"—teachers who had been there for decades and were extremely reluctant to question their beliefs and actions. *This is the way math class has operated for years. Why change it now?* On the other side, you had the younger teachers in their twenties who never seemed to make it to more than two or three years before becoming so discouraged that they moved on to somewhere else. Both sides were weary (and wary) of whatever The District was going to do to them next.

Continued →

→ *Continued*

These camps became particularly divided over curriculum. My first year there, the elementary schools were choosing a curriculum (out of three) that they would "adopt" for the next few years. Nothing exposes philosophical divisions quite like asking 75 elementary school teachers to come to a consensus on the same curriculum. It got ugly.

I came to know the curriculum they used quite well. I won't name it, but it has a reputation for being a tragic combination of (a) positioning students as passive consumers of math who follow their teacher along, filling out "I do, we do, you do" workspaces in their textbooks and (b) using scripted math lessons that position teachers to "walk students through" the content.

Most elementary teachers liked the curriculum:

> *I love this textbook. The lesson planning is a breeze. I just walk them through it really. And look at all the practice problems! My students need so much practice, you know, to get them caught up and ready for the standardized tests. The curriculum also comes with these bins of manipulatives. But I never use them. They just become a needless distraction and slow me down from my pacing plan. Besides, students are not allowed to use them on the standardized test, so why should I teach them how to use them in class?*

A significant minority of them didn't like the curriculum, and a few loathed it:

> *This textbook destroys our students' love of mathematics and our love of teaching it. There are no rich tasks in here. There's nothing meaningful for them to think about. Can we please go with either of the other curriculum options on the table? No? If you're going to make me use this, can I at least have the manipulative you're not going to use?*

The curriculum became a useful device for The District to establish a common pacing plan, design common assessments, and keep track of "student achievement data" as they monitored progress toward The Test. There was a lot of pressure to keep to these pacing plans. In an effort to focus on the core content of each grade level, all the "measurement and data" and "statistics and probability" content strands were pushed to the end of the calendar year—in other words, they were never taught. *That stuff isn't on the test that much so we don't need to teach it.*

Anne and Carol

In these content-focused Gardens, teaching became more about efficiency and answer getting. And this discouraged quite a few teachers, teachers like Anne and Carol. The day I spent with them will serve as a major window for our work in Part 3. There is a lot to look through with this window, and I invite you to discuss what you see and how you see it with your colleagues in your next Campfire Gathering.

The Morning With Anne and Carol

Anne, Carol, and I spent the morning getting to know each other. I invited the principal to be with us. Unfortunately, he had a "full plate" that day, but would "pop in" whenever he could. *Trust me. You'll see things about your teachers' professional learning needs you haven't seen before.* My plea was no more effective than my invitation. He would "do what he could."

The three of us talked about our passions and our vision of what an ideal math classroom looks like. I had never seen them teach—we had only known each other for about an hour—but we had been able to build enough rapport that they began opening up about their Dump.

Anne: *I have a group of students in my class who always keep shouting out answers and it's interrupting the learning of others. The math is just too easy—they can figure it out because they already know their math facts. And I feel bad for them. They're bored. But I also get really angry at them. They're like a pack of academic bullies—they think they're better than everyone else. And it's not fair to the others. They have a right to learn too.*

Carol begins to open up: *Hearing you Anne, I'm wondering if the same thing has been happening in my room too. I sense that a lot of my students sit there quietly and wait for the same students to carry the cognitive load for them. I used to think it was laziness on their part, but now I'm wondering if my quiet students don't feel safe or comfortable speaking up. It's something I need to observe more closely.*

I spend time mirroring what they have to say because this is something they clearly have strong feelings about. We go back and forth a few times, each time I try to mirror back until I'm able to accurately capture what they are trying to say. I want to understand the issues that are most important to them before moving forward, and to do that, I need to help them clarify their beliefs *with* them, not *for* them.

Continued →

→ Continued

> Me: *Something I hear you value is the importance that all students have a chance to share their thinking in math class. And you're feeling discouraged because you're sensing some hierarchy forming—some students are diminishing the voices of others. And you're looking for an action that will help you change that story?*
>
> They agree.

Stepping Out of the Textbook

Anne and Carol were in the division unit and their next lesson was titled "Using Equal Groups to Solve Division Problems." This would be only the third lesson these students have had on the concept of "division"—one of the major focus strands for third graders. The lesson opens with this task:

> *Jessica has 24 large apples. She wants to make 8 loaves of apple bread. How many apples should she put in each loaf?*

In the teacher guide, the lesson plan asks teachers to have students count out 24 counting cubes to model the situation. In the student workbook, there are eight circles already drawn on the page for students to distribute the 24 counting cubes into eight groups of three.

We take the action to convert the textbook task into the Numberless Word Problem you'll see in just a moment. Our intent was to find ways to position all of Anne's learners so they could make sense of the problem before solving it—and this meant finding a way to keep the "answer-shouters" engaged in thought with their classmates. The best way to keep "answer-shouters" at bay is to present a math problem so there's no "right answer," or better yet, a math problem that doesn't have a question at all—until the students ask them. Carol also makes the suggestion to change "loaves" to "pies" in order to help some of the language learners in the classroom.

Here is a basic sketch of the lesson plan:

- ▶ Workbooks would stay inside their desks to start class. Students would spend 15-20 minutes in discourse about the Numberless Word Problem prompts.

> After that, Anne was going to ask the students to get out their workbooks, and the lesson plan would follow what was in the textbook. Students could work ahead if they wanted to while Anne monitored the learning progress of the students who needed more time making equal groups with manipulatives.

We knew it wasn't the best lesson plan, but it was the best we could do in the time we had. And it kept Anne more at ease knowing that she wasn't falling further behind the pacing plan.

While Anne taught the lesson, Carol and I observed The Group of "answer-shouters." We sat next to each other with a piece of paper between us so that we could record and share data and also silently exchange some quick thoughts with each other during the lesson. *What do you see? How do you see it?* We were careful not to sit too close to The Group because we knew our presence would change their behavior. We positioned ourselves far enough away but close enough that we could eavesdrop to get the vantage we needed.

Miguel and His 100 Apples

Just before arriving, the substitute in Anne's room had told students that we were coming in to teach a math lesson. When we walked into the room, most students had, by habit, taken their workbooks out. *This is what we always do in "math class."*

Anne: *Thanks for getting out your books. So prepared! I love it! But today I am going to ask that we put away our textbooks and do something a little different. Can everyone please get out a blank piece of paper and something to write with instead?*

Most of the students follow directions, but not The Group. They look anxious, fidgety, and start whispering to each other. They don't quite know how to handle the position they're in. For a moment, they're the least cooperative students in the room. *What are we doing? Why aren't we using our textbooks? What's going on here? This is what we normally do.* They're bothered. We've interrupted their mental model about how math class is supposed to go.

Anne intentionally ignores this data. Her job is to focus on implementing the task in a way that promotes reasoning. It's our job to watch The Group and collect data to talk about later.

Anne: *Today we are going to be math detectives together as we figure out what information is missing from this problem. Can y'all help me out?*

Continued →

→ Continued

Students nod. She displays an image on the board showing the bolded text below, a picture of a basket of apples, and a picture of an apple pie.

Read with me while I read aloud. **Jessica used several large apples to make some pies.** *Hmmmm. What math do you see in this sentence? I'll give you some quiet think time, and then you'll have a chance to share with your group.*

During wait time, The Group is very confused. *Has our teacher lost her mind? There's no math in that sentence!! This isn't what a math problem is supposed to look like. Where are the numbers? What question am I supposed to answer? This is stupid.* They're uncooperative—not defiant, but resistant, reluctant.

From groups around the room, we hear students focus on the words "several" and "some." One student blurts out, *Well, how many apples does she have?* Students in The Group sit with arms crossed and don't speak.

Anne calls the class back to attention and asks for students to share their thoughts. Next to each comment she writes the student's name.

Mio: *If she used smaller apples, she'd need to have more of them.*

Britney: *Some pies means that there has to be more than one pie.*

Jamal's group: *Someone at my table said there has to be more apples than there are pies.*

Anne: *Are we ready for the next clue?* Students nod.

Jessica used several large apples to make some pies. She used the same number of apples in each pie. *How does this new clue change what you already know?*

A short pause for silent think time before students start discussion. This time students in The Group begin to perk up a bit. *Maybe there is some math here, after all.*

Gina: *It's a multiplication problem.*

Rory: *No! It's a division problem.*

Asking for evidence, Anne draws out from students that this problem involves "equal groups," a concept they learned from the previous unit on multiplication.

Here's the next clue: **Jessica used 24 large apples to make some pies. She used the same number of apples in each pie.** *How does this clue change what you already know?*

More student discussion. Things move more rapidly as students seem to be making sense of the problem. We see students nod as these questions are written on the board.

Hank: *How many pies did she make?*

Maria: *How many apples will she use for each pie?*

Students in The Group start to engage more. The interplay between their identity and agency shifts from "I can't do this—I won't do this" to "I can do this—I want more."

Before continuing on to the last clue, Anne invites students to make an estimation. *How many pies do you think she could make with 24 apples? Can anyone come up with a reasonable guess?* Student answers vary, but most seem to think it's somewhere between 2 and 12.

*Last Clue: **Jessica used 24 large apples to make 8 pies. She used the same number of apples for each pie**. What mathematical questions can we ask about this problem?*

At this point, students seem to all be on the same page: *How many apples can she use for each pie?* But then one student speaks up: *What if she had a 100 apples? How many pies could she make then?*

You might think that a student in The Group asked the "100 Apples" question. It wasn't. It was a student named Miguel who, according to Anne, rarely speaks in class and keeps pretty much to himself. Anne recorded it on the chart and wrote "Miguel's question" next to it.

Anne: *I love this question Miguel, but we don't have time for it today. We need to solve this problem instead. So can everybody get out your counting cubes for—*

Can I figure out Miguel's question?

This stops Anne in her tracks. One of the "answer-shouters" had already turned into a "question-shouter." *Improvement!* She looks at us. I give her my best nonverbal "why not?" expression that also says "your call." To Anne's credit, she embraces the Art of Not Knowing.

Sure. You can do that.

Well, can I do it too? . . . Yeah, me too . . . I like Miguel's question better.

The proverbial can of worms has been opened. She looks at me—*What do I do with this data, now?*

I invite her to come over to us with a subtle wave. We have a quick huddle in the back of the room. What are students doing during this 30-second exchange? They're watching us—that's what they always do. Besides, this was probably the most exciting thing to go down in math class in a while.

Me: *What options are you considering?*

Anne: *I want to let them do that, but what about the lesson we planned?*

Continued →

→ Continued

> Me: *You're worried about falling behind on the pacing plan?*
>
> Anne: *Yeah. And what about the students that really need to work with the manipulatives?*
>
> Carol: *I can help out if you want me to.*
>
> Me: *What is your Tree telling you to do right now?*
>
> From our morning session, I knew Anne to be an Artist and a Conductor. She shared stories about how she liked to try new things and was confident with coordinating learning and adjusting on the fly. I knew she was capable. As her colleague, my job was to show her that.
>
> Anne looks at her students. Forty-six eyes stare back at her. But not Miguel's. He's figuring out how many pies Jessica can make with 100 apples. In our reflection later, she remembers feeling *God bless that sweet child. What does he need right now?* It was the sight of seeing him, in that moment, that gave Anne the vantage to find the courage to do what she did next.
>
> Anne (quietly, to us): *To hell with the damn pacing plan.*
>
> Returning to the front of the room, she offers a suggestion. *How about we work on both problems, and you can choose which one?* Students cheer—literally.
>
> *OK. How should we organize ourselves so that we can do that?*

More Than 33, but Less Than 34

The next 20 minutes was "math class" at its finest. Turns out, almost all of them wanted to solve Miguel's problem. Depending on the solution strategy, the 100 apples question could be approached as a division problem involving a remainder, a topic usually reserved for fourth grade, or it could be approached as a proportional reasoning question and indicative of the thinking we ask sixth and seventh graders to do.

It was fascinating watching them work—identity enhanced, agency ignited—*unafraid* because they had no reason to be. They didn't know it wasn't third grade math. And it was all spontaneous—one of those magical "math moments" that could never be contrived. And it's a moment that wouldn't happen in a content-focused Garden. *We don't have time for your brilliant question Miguel. We have to solve this textbook problem instead.*

Can That Be True?

At this point, Carol and I abandoned our data collection duties. Carol sought out some students who wanted to work on the original question with 24 apples. I took on the role of encouraging students to share their thinking with each other and show them how to select other co-think partners.

- *Hmmm. I heard Cindy and Maria talking about the same thing—maybe you can ask them?*

- *Looks like you're trying the same approach as that group over there—can we walk over together and see what they have to say?*

- *Miguel seems to have an idea—how about you go ask him what he's thinking?*

Three main solution strategies emerged:

- Some students counted out a hundred cubes and made groups of three until they ended up with one left over. *What does that mean? Why is it left over?*

- Another group didn't use the manipulatives but used repeated addition with pencil and paper. *Three plus three is six. Plus three more is nine. Plus three is 12 . . .*

- Another group explored Miguel's "doubling method." His brain saw the whole situation differently—he saw it as ratios between apples and pies. He didn't know what ratios were called, but he was using them intuitively, creating his own ratio table along the way.

    Anne: *This is really interesting, can you tell me what you got here, Miguel?*

    Miguel: *I call it my doubling strategy.*

    Can you tell me how it works?

    Well, 24 apples is 8 pies. 48 apples is 16 pies. 96 apples is 32 pies.

    Interesting. Now what?

    I don't know. If I keep going it's too much. And 96 isn't enough apples.

    You're stuck?

    Yeah.

Continued →

→ Continued

> Y'know, your doubling strategy is pretty cool, Miguel. I bet some students in the room would love to learn about it. Can we share it with the class? Maybe they can help you get unstuck.
>
> The last data I saw in the classroom was Miguel teaching others about his "doubling strategy"—butts out of seats, all huddled forward, as if they were all saying: *Teach me, Miguel. I'm curious.* At that moment, I looked up—the principal and the "District Chief of Data" had walked in at some point. I didn't know how long they'd been there, but they didn't look pleased and asked that I step outside. As I walked out of the room, I heard someone in Miguel's group say, *There's four apples left. Three make another pie.* Another student: *And we have an extra apple.* And another student: *So it's more than 33 and less than 34? Can that be true?*

What Do You Need to See to Change Your Mind?

My grandfather had this aphorism: *Never miss a good opportunity to be quiet.* His point: *Sometimes it's more productive to keep your mouth shut.* As I've gotten older, I've learned the power of this wisdom—as a teacher, colleague, friend, and partner. When we're quiet, we can listen.

And then there are times when—because of our position—*we must speak up.* Facing Chief of Data and the principal outside Anne's classroom was one of those positions. I had nothing to lose—but Anne and Carol did, and so did Miguel and the rest of the students at Headwinds Unified. If I sound cheeky in the conversation I'm about to share, I was. If I sound irreverent and mildly antagonistic, I was. I knew what I had to say wasn't going to matter much—but it felt important that I say it. The Chief of Data had just been promoted the previous summer. In her previous position as a principal, she was not a fan of my lesson study work. *You can't show me this collaborative approach to professional learning raises test scores, Chase. And until you do, I don't want you wasting my teachers' time. They have more important things to do. We are trying to become the first "Distinguished School" in The District.* To her credit, she succeeded in achieving this distinction. It's one of the reasons why she got promoted.

And now the writing was on the wall. My days were numbered.

What Do You Need to See to Change Your Mind?

Chief of Data: *What is going on in there? This is not what we expected to see in a math classroom.*

Me: *Isn't it great? We didn't expect it to happen either. What did you see?*

Chief of Data: *I see students not sitting in their seats and not listening to a teacher. I see students not using their textbooks. All in a classroom with a teacher that hasn't shown improvement in test scores over the past three years. I ask again, what is going on in there?*

Me: *I saw the same data. And Anne mentioned the test scores this morning. Trust me, she's worried about them too—and it's only October, can you believe it? Now, what else did you see in that classroom? Because if that's it, I think we had two very different lived experiences just now . . .*

The principal was a little nonplussed by my language. But not Chief of Data. She knew what nourished my Tree. And I knew what nourished hers. This was not our first time at this particular rodeo debating what math class should look like.

Me, getting emotional: *Did you see Miguel and his brilliance? Did you see students unafraid of math? Did you catch how most of the students in there are going beyond what their crappy textbook asked them to do? Did you see a teacher exercise her courage, her conviction to follow what her teaching soul told her was the just thing to do in her position? Or did you not see any of that?*

Chief of Data, calm and collected as always: *Look Chase. We talked about this last year and the year before. There's no research that says what you're doing works. And despite you being here for more than three years, test scores are not going up. I appreciate your effort, but it's not working.*

The bell rings. The school day is over. Anne's classroom door opens and her students start pouring out. Filled with energy and joy. Miguel walking tall—beaming. *That was fun, Mr. Chase. Can we do it again?*

Me: *I hope so Miguel! Never stop asking questions in class, OK? You were a math hero today.*

Other students peppered us with verbal data as they walked by. *Yeah. I liked math class today. We got to be out of our seats! And work together! Can you believe that we were doing middle school math today? It was cool.*

Continued →

→ *Continued*

Anne and Carol come out. They look winded—and elated. Anne's face falls a bit when she sees Chief of Data, her former principal.

Me: *How did it go?*

Anne: *We lost track of time and didn't finish.*

Me: *Imperfect and unfinished is the best way to be. Can't wait to hear all about it in our reflection later.*

As Anne and Carol walk away, Chief of Data: *See? They didn't even finish the lesson because of you. They have to be giving students their exit tickets. It's the data we want teachers to be using every day to monitor student progress toward mastery.*

Me: *Did you not just hear all that data? Did you not just feel the joy? At what point do we stop treating our students like they're test scores that need to be raised? We're destroying their relationship with math. What do you need to see to change your mind?*

KEY TAKEAWAYS FOR CHAPTER 8

✴ We will look through this window throughout the rest of Part 3. For now, I position you as being capable of drawing your own Key Takeaways for Chapter 8 and to talk about them in your Campfire Gatherings. This is not a cop-out. The most important takeaways right now are your own, and I don't want to taint them.

INTERLUDE 8:
ACTIONS TO POSITION
LEARNERS AS CAPABLE

In Part 3, the Interludes contain multiple invitations to continue embodying the Core Elements of Deliberate Practice. Lighthouse Reflections will contain questions to focus and reflect on your beliefs and question the actions you're currently taking. Seek Vantages will offer invitations to gain the perspective you need to refine and calibrate your craft and help sustain your flourishment. Last, Campfire Gatherings will consist of a variety of invitations to share, listen, and reflect on the learning we are making together as active partners in each other's professional growth.

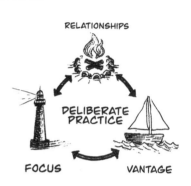

I encourage you to keep coming back to these activities throughout the months and years to come. More important, I hope you learn to improve and add to these stories with your own truth. And in the months ahead, I invite you to share them with others and be effective windows and active partners in each other's professional flourishment. Remember, you are an author of our story just as much as I am.

LIGHTHOUSE REFLECTION 5: AN INVITATION TO REFLECT ON HOW YOU POSITION YOUR STUDENTS

FOCUS

Position is a word rich with meaning. It represents a location. *Timur placed his queen in a powerful position on the chessboard.* It's a situation of circumstance—especially as it relates to one's agency. *What am I supposed to do with Rudy in my position?* It represents someone's point of view. *I have a strong position about the ways we treat our students like test scores.*

Position is also a verb—it's something we can do to things, including ourselves and our students. Lighthouse Reflection 5 is an invitation to reflect on how you position your students in your classroom. The intent is that these questions are something that you return to throughout your journey. They are not intended to be answered in a single sitting. Like previous Lighthouse Reflections, your thoughts and reactions to these prompts can be fuel for future Campfire Gatherings.

How we position our learners significantly affects the outcomes of the learning experience—for both students and teachers. To show you what I mean, here are two stories about teaching someone how to drive, which serve as an analogy for how we position our students in math class.

> ### How we position our learners significantly affects the outcomes of the learning experience—for both students and teachers.

As you read, I invite you to focus on the following questions:

- In what ways are the learners positioned as being capable? What actions do the learners take in their position?

- In what ways is my dad positioned? What outcomes does he achieve from his position?

- What might be some takeaways from this window about how you position your students and yourselves in the learning process in the math classroom? ●

Learning to Drive: Position in the Content-Focused Approach

When I was 14, I asked my dad if he'd teach me to drive on the farm property. He said yes. We hopped in "Uncle Buck"—a pea-green 1970 Chevy Impala—with me behind the wheel and my dad in the passenger seat. And I thought we were ready to go. *I'm in position!*

Dad: *A vehicle will kill you if you don't know what you're doing, son. Before we start, there's a few things I want you to know about how a car works. You can't just get in the thing and drive.*

Me, to myself: *Uh-oh. Here we go.*

Forty-five minutes later, we're in the same position—Uncle Buck had not moved. My eyes had glazed over 20 minutes ago. We had gone over different positions of the ignition switch. On. Accessories. Start. Off. What the different dashboard lights mean when they come on. *If the brake light comes on, it could mean one of three things. The first thing it could mean . . . .* Shifting of gears. Gear ratios. Uphill. Downhill. Engine braking. Emergency braking. Even how the carburetor worked. *It's not a gas pedal so much as it is an air pedal—when you step on it, you're drawing more air in and that creates the vacuum that draws in the fuel.*

I finally lost my patience and got out of the car. *I get it dad. But I don't even want to do this anymore.*

Learning to Drive: Position in the Story-Focused Approach

Twenty years later, one of my dad's grandsons, Riley, wants to learn to drive. Not wanting the lad to go through the same experience from my childhood, I intervened.

We had an old pickup on the farm at the time. It would start in gear without the clutch engaged—turn the key while the manual transmission was in first gear, the engine would fire up and immediately the truck would move. And in first gear, it didn't matter how hard you stomped on the brakes. The front wheels would lock up and skid, but those back tires would just keep churning until you pressed in the clutch or turned the key off.

Me: Hey dad. I know you wanted me to internalize that vehicles can kill me if I don't know what I'm doing, but I think I have an idea that will put Riley in a better position to learn that. It'll also put you in a position to help him understand what you want him to know—instead of getting out and walking away like I did. Let's point that old pickup out into the field. Make sure he can't hit anything. And tell him if he turns the key, the engine will start. Wouldn't that teach him the same thing, just from a different position?

My dad didn't say anything. He didn't need to. He understood my point: position the learner.

Everything went according to plan. They both hopped in, Riley turned the key, and off they went. Immediately panicked, Riley does the instinctual thing—step on the brakes. But that doesn't work. *What should I do?! What should I do?!*

Figure it out! You wanted to learn to drive, Riley. First lesson: A vehicle can kill you if you don't know what you're doing. What are you going to do now?

The old pickup keeps growling forward at a walking speed. At any time, my dad could reach over and turn the key off, but he wanted Riley to learn from his position—not necessarily about driving but about himself and his instincts as a driver. Better to have him panicking for the first time in a safe situation in a hay field instead of at freeway speeds when his life, and the lives of those around him, are on the line.

Riley eventually stops his screaming. And he stops stepping on the brakes, gains a bit more control over his emotions, assesses his options . . . and starts driving.

There are some activities in life where we need to be very careful how we position children and young adults so they don't harm themselves as they learn. Swimming, rock climbing, welding, and driving on the road are good examples. We don't want to position them to "just figure it out on their own" when it comes to these things—some sort of gradual release of responsibility is required for safety.

Learning mathematics is not like learning to swim, rock climb, weld, or drive on the road—but we often act like it is. I invite us to think about how Riley was positioned as capable and having ownership over his learning experience and how we can do that *more* for our students in our classroom. I invite us to do *much less* of the gradual release of responsibility model because no one ever hurts themselves doing math—it's actually a pretty safe activity.

> *I invite us to do much less of the gradual release of responsibility model because no one ever hurts themselves doing math—it's actually a pretty safe activity.*

Note
The "gradual release of responsibility" is often called "I do, we do, you do." It is often what happens when we are "walking our students" through the textbook.

When we gradually release responsibility, the authority for the learning, at least in the beginning, is all on us, the teacher. When we do this regularly, we are showing our students that we don't believe they are capable. And we also risk losing their interest because we're not giving them direct experiences with mathematics and an opportunity to know more about their instincts as mathematicians.

Too many times in my career, my students said the same thing as I did to my dad because I didn't position them in ways that let them experience the richness of mathematics. *I get it Mr. O, but I don't want to learn this anymore.* Of all the actions I invite us to question in this Interlude, this is perhaps the most important: let's examine how we're positioning our students so that they can experience mathematics and demonstrate their capabilities. I invite us to do much less of the "gradual release of responsibility" approach to teaching so we can create space to practice the other actions in the Interludes in Part 3.

QUESTIONS TO FOCUS YOUR THINKING

FOCUS

What does it mean "to position your students as capable" in your own words?

What actions are you currently taking to position your students as capable? How are you showing them that you value their thinking?

Where is your expertise falling short? What does it look like in your Garden when you're not able to position your students as capable?

What story making is resulting from the positions you've created as a teacher? What changes are you considering in your actions and routines? ●

Positioning Your Students as Capable

In my years since leaving the classroom, I had the opportunity to be a lead author of a comprehensive middle school math curriculum. And through that lens, I have learned that we rely too heavily on textbooks to help us "walk students through a math lesson." In a content-focused Garden, it becomes extremely challenging to position students as learners who can see themselves as mathematically capable, competent, and curious. And it can likewise be extremely challenging to position ourselves in ways that we can share authority with them, elevate their voice, and foster their sense of mathematical agency. In a story-focused Garden that prioritizes student identity and agency, we recognize that mathematics is not something that one learns best from a textbook. It's something we learn best when our curiosity is piqued, and we feel invited to share our thinking and our questions. Miguel's "100 apples" question probably doesn't happen in a content-focused Garden where a teacher is walking them through the textbook.

It's been my perspective that the Headwinds have conditioned educators to expect too much out of the textbook we use. I invite us to interrogate our beliefs about textbooks and question our actions using them in our lessons for two reasons:

1. **There is no textbook that will meet all students' and teachers' needs.** All curriculum writers face the challenge to create authentic learning moments for students and teachers they have never met and will never see. They do their best, but this is an impossible task, because so much about the art of math teaching and learning is personal to our lived experiences. If there was a magic bullet that met all of our students' learning needs, we'd all be using it. It simply doesn't exist.

2. **Just because it's written in your textbook doesn't mean it's good for student learning.** Even curriculum writers would rarely teach a lesson they wrote the exact way it is written. We know that so much of teaching math is about spontaneity and relationships that cannot

be contrived. We also know writing curriculum comes with constraints of its own (from the publisher, from the market, from standards, and legislation) and is never perfect—even in our own eyes.

A story-focused Garden empowers and *requires* us to use the textbook as only one tool in our toolbox, and to use it flexibly, enhancing it with our own knowledge of our students in order to position students as capable. Sometimes it requires modifying what is in our textbook, and sometimes it requires stepping outside of it altogether.

Actions to Position Your Students as Capable

Here are some actions that you can take to position your students as capable. All of these actions and resources below require us to step out of our textbooks—at least a little bit. You may even use your textbook as a starting point as you plan, but we must be willing, like Anne and Carol, to see what happens when we start our lessons with textbooks closed.

1. **Show students you value their lived experiences and what they already know.**
   With any mathematical task that has a context, you can ask the following question: *Tell me what you know about _____. What questions do you have about the topic?* To get students comfortable, start with nonmathematical aspects of the context, For example: *Tell me what you know about bridges. Sound. The solar system. Apples and pies. Voting. Credit cards. Musical notes. And what questions do you have about the topic?*
   This cultural practice shows students they are capable of participating and contributing to the discussion. From this position, start adding mathematical questions that help keep them engaged with the mathematics in the task. *Tell me what you know about fractions. The number 12. Linear functions. Slope. Triangles. Area and volume. What questions do you have about the topic?*

2. **Tell stories and introduce situations using visuals.**
   All students are capable of telling stories, interpreting the stories of others, and looking at a visual and having something to say. Think of ways to introduce your textbook tasks with stories from your own lived experiences and/or use visuals that invite your students to share stories about their own related lived experiences.

3. **Create information gaps that offer your students something they can all wonder about.**
   We saw Anne do this with her Numberless Word Problem. By hiding the numbers and the question, she is able to create information gaps that ignite her students' curiosity. We create the need for student questioning. When we present all the information at once and give

the question to the students, there's nothing to be curious about. It immediately becomes a word problem that must be solved and our students are positioned as answer-getters as we saw in the story above. When we create information gaps, we can begin to address a common dilemma: *How do I engage students who already know the answer to the math problem in the textbook I'm teaching?*

Think of ways you can modify the tasks in your book to create more information gaps. Hide the numbers and slowly reveal them like a Numberless Word Problem. Hide the question so there's no answer at first—just a situation to discuss and ask questions about. When looking at graphs that have a context, consider hiding the title, labels, and/ or scale for each axis and invite students to consider: *What might be a story for this graph?*

4. Seek out some low-floor, high-leverage instructional routines such as those listed here.

Links to these instructional routines can be found in the Campfire Gathering Facilitation Guide for Campfire Gathering 5.

- Numberless Word Problems
- Slow Reveal Graphs
- Notice and Wonder
- Which One Doesn't Belong
- Number Talks (or Math Talks or Algebra Talks)
- Number Talks With Images
- Would You Rather Math
- 101 Questions
- Graphing Stories
- Debate Math
- What's the Same/Different?
- Estimation 180
- 3-Act Math Tasks

FURTHER LEARNING

On-Your-Feet Guide: Modifying Mathematical Tasks: Eight Strategies to Engage Students in Thinking and Reasoning by Smith et al. (2020) is an excellent resource for specific actions that can deepen your practice of stepping out of the textbook.

online resources **Further Your Craft:** Learn more about these actions and download resources at bit.ly/3o7bBzq, or visit the *The Imperfect and Unfinished Math Teacher* Free Resources tab on the Corwin website. These actions are things you can deliberately observe in each other's math lessons during Seek Vantages and talk about in your Campfire Gatherings.

SEEK VANTAGE 5: NEW EYES ON HOW YOUR STUDENTS ARE POSITIONED

VANTAGE

The protocols for Seek Vantages will become more informal as you learn how to guide your own learning as active partners in each other's professional learning. The purpose of this observation is to help you refine and calibrate your practice of positioning students as capable learners.

I invite you to choose one of the actions from the previous list and commit to practicing it. You may choose the same one as a group or you can each focus on different ones. Regardless, spend time in each other's classrooms watching each other take deliberate actions to position your students as capable thinkers and doers in math class.

I invite you to have informal huddles, much like the one Anne, Carol, and I engaged in, and ask yourselves these questions to each other while the lesson is going on.

How are students positioned in the classroom?

What do you notice?

What might I want to consider as I move forward with this lesson?

What missed opportunities do you see?

How might I position more students in ways that they can demonstrate to themselves they are capable?

Remember, like all things in this book, this list is not a recipe. It is imperfect and unfinished. ●

CAMPFIRE GATHERING 5: AGENDAS TO FURTHER YOUR CRAFT OF POSITIONING STUDENTS AS CAPABLE

RELATIONSHIPS

As you evolve, individually and collectively, your Campfire Gatherings must evolve as well. I invite you to keep using the Facilitation Guide and empower you to create your own agendas as you see fit.

In the Facilitation Guide for Campfire Gathering 5, you will find links to the instructional routines listed in Interlude 8. You will also find some suggested agenda activities that you and your colleagues can implement to help each other improve your expertise of positioning your students as capable mathematical thinkers and doers. ●

NOTES

_____

_____

_____

_____

_____

_____

_____

_____

_____

_____

_____

_____

_____

_____

_____

_____

9

FOUR EQUITY ACTIONS FOR THE STORY-FOCUSED TEACHER

Where We've Been

In Chapter 8, we read a story about Anne and Carol's struggles to cultivate a story-focused Garden at Headwinds Unified School District. This story will be used as a window throughout Part 3.

Where We're Going

In Chapter 9, you will be invited to test your beliefs about your professional identity and question your actions when it comes to thinking about and implementing "equity actions." We will also explore what we gain when we shift from a "content-focused" Garden to a "story-focused" Garden.

Human beings are creatures of interpretation. Our behavior and our attitudes are shaped by our mental models: the images, assumptions, and stories that we carry in our minds of ourselves, other people, institutions, and every aspect of the world. Differences between mental models explain why two people can observe the same event and describe it differently: They are paying attention to different details. The core task of the discipline *of mental models is to bring tacit assumptions and attitudes to the surface so people can explore and talk about their differences and misunderstandings with minimal defensiveness.*

—Senge, Schools That Learn
(2012, pp. 99–100)

Why We Haven't Defined Equity

Since Interlude 3 and throughout our journey, I have invited you to think about your vision of equity—the ideal math classroom that you are trying to achieve with your teaching expertise. And you probably have noticed that I have not defined "equity" explicitly for us.

I haven't because I trust that you already have an internal understanding of what equity means. Every human does. And that's where every teacher's journey starts—with their own imperfect and unfinished understanding of what an equitable math classroom can look, sound, and feel like. And as I have tried to show you through all these chapters, furthering our teaching expertise *requires* us to have an understanding of equity that *remains* imperfect and unfinished. Equity is a concept with a meaning that we must let evolve for ourselves on our journey of reflecting, calibrating, and collaborating.

Equity is a concept with a meaning that we must let ourselves evolve for ourselves on our journey of reflecting, calibrating, and collaborating.

When we focus on defining words and concepts such as "equity," "equitable teaching," and an "equitable math class," we risk creating the following beliefs and actions that are *unproductive* to expanding our potential and furthering our expertise:

▶ We assume that because we've all read the definition or discussed the same research article, we have the same understanding of the meaning of the word. (We don't.)

▶ The meanings of words never change. (They do—and they should, because we change.)

In this chapter, we'll unpack these points and then test two essential beliefs about our professional identity. I will invite us to do the following:

1. Think of ourselves *less* as people who teach mathematics content to students and *more* as cultural stewards who help our students author their own math stories.

2. Spend *less* time defining what equity is and *more* time co-creating a vision of what equity can look/sound/feel like in a story-focused Garden.

As is true with all the beliefs and actions that I invite us to test and question, none of this is a magical recipe nor are they commandments. I'm simply inviting us to do *less* of one thing so we can do *more* of another. I will be very explicit about when I invite us to *stop* doing something like I am right now.

I'm explicitly asking us to *stop* viewing effective math teaching and our journey to furthering our expertise as something that can be brought about by following a recipe or completing a checklist. *This book is not a recipe.* Improving our craft requires us to abandon our habit of hoping that some external solution exists out there in the world—some "magic bullet"—that will vanquish all our teaching woes. It's simply not there. The solution is within us—and it is within the students we teach. This is the first Beacon—the transformation we need must come from the inside-out.

Words Are Stories: Their Meaning Transcends Their Definitions

Is a Hot Dog a Sandwich?

A few summers ago, this question was a hot topic among my colleagues on Twitter. I've heard teachers say that they had been using it as an effective way to start constructive debate in a math classroom as students critique arguments with counterexamples and work together to create a common, concise, and coherent definition of what "sandwich" means. For example, a discussion might go like this:

> A hot dog is a sandwich because it has bread and meat.

> What about peanut butter and jelly sandwiches? They don't have meat. Is a peanut butter and jelly not a sandwich?

A hot dog isn't a sandwich because it has only one piece of bread, and a sandwich is supposed to have two.

What about a hoagie or a sub? They're sandwiches and like hot dogs, they only have one piece of bread.

So does that mean a taco is also a sandwich?

If a taco is a sandwich then so is a burrito.

To me, there was value to the question beyond its use as a prompt in the math classroom, but I couldn't put my finger on it. That summer, on a trip to reconnect with some old high school friends, I brought this question up to see what they thought of it. I wanted to hear the vantage of nonteachers as they discussed this question.

At one point in the conversation, my friend Kyle said, *Look. I'll grant you that a hot dog is a sandwich. But if you offered to make me a sandwich and then gave me a hot dog, I would be a bit taken aback because it's not what I'd expect to see. It doesn't fit my mental model of what a sandwich should be.*

Boom. Thank you, Kyle. Just the vantage I needed.

When we ask whether or not a hot dog is a sandwich, we invite a playful conversation that allows us to debate the meaning of a word. To a large degree, each and every one of us is entitled to their own definition of what a sandwich is and what a sandwich is not. Few of us are offended because, unless you're *really* attached to your beliefs about food categories, nobody cares that much. We can both live comfortable lives being friends despite steadfast differences on this topic. The worst thing that happens is what Kyle says. *This doesn't look like the thing I thought we were talking about.*

The "sandwich" question exposes us to a greater truth about the language we use with each other. The meaning of words is not found in their definitions so much as they are found in the stories—the lived experiences—we attach to these words. And as we have seen, because our lived experiences are what make us unique, our understanding of words have subtle, unique differences as well.

> Because our lived experiences are what make us unique, our understanding of words have subtle, unique differences as well.

Sandwich. Dog. Family. Thanksgiving. College. Eggplant parmesan. Love.

You read those words, I imagine we are seeing similar things but we are not seeing the same thing, in part, because we have had different lived experiences. With "sandwich" words like these, our differences are easy to celebrate, and we can appreciate the uniqueness we bring to the conversation—if we pause and give space for us to share the stories behind the meaning of these words, that is.

Liberal. Conservative. Police. Voting rights. Border wall. Impeachment.

These are often difficult words to talk about because the meaning we attach to them are heavily influenced by our emotional attachment to our lived experience and our identities. These are not "sandwich" words—they are words where "being right" *really matters to us*. Debating the definitions of these words is often unproductive and divisive because the mental models we attach to them are deeply woven into our individual and collective identities. Because they are very *political* and *cultural*, the meaning we attach to these words—the stories—are unlikely to change *even if we talk about them*.

Is "equity" a "sandwich" word?

Our understanding of equity in the math classroom is heavily influenced by our lived experiences and the mental models we have about our professional identity and the work we do. It's even influenced by our own math story as a student. And, in a culture established by the Headwinds, I don't think "equity" (or "math class" for that matter) are "sandwich" words nearly as much as we might think. Like "fairness," "justice," and "equality," the meaning we attach to "equity" is very subjective and personal—and we are attached to our beliefs about it. We need to be careful about how we go about defining what "equity" means so that we don't get hung up on "being right."

Like "fairness," "justice," and "equality," the meaning we attach to "equity" is very subjective and personal— and we are attached to our beliefs about it.

We Must Let Our Meanings of Words Evolve

A "phone" is perhaps the most ideal example of how much our understanding of a word can change over time as our lived experience with it changes. As a child in the 1930s, my father walked down the street to a neighbor's house to use the phone—and there weren't many people with phones to call back then. Now he's almost 90 years old, and a farmer with a smartphone in his pocket that he can use to contact virtually anyone on the planet whenever he wants. As our mental model of the phone changed over time, it's changed our *fundamental identity as humans*—individually, culturally, globally. That's an impressive story for a single word. It's an ideal example of both how elaborate our mental models can be and how much they can evolve over time when they are woven into a common shared lived experience. Because, liberal or conservative, we can all agree we have evolved together—phones and humans.

Phone. Marriage. Masks. Pandemic. Marijuana.

All of these words have changed significantly in our lifetimes because our lived experiences with these words have changed. Marriage isn't just for heterosexuals. Masks are no longer just for bank robbers, medical professionals, and Halloween costumes. Pandemics are no longer just riveting fodder for sci-fi movie plots. Even marijuana has emerged from the propaganda of *Reefer Madness* and the political "War on Drugs" to be something that is, depending on where you live these days, an integrated part of everyday life. *What would Nixon say now?* It's incredible how much our collective understanding of words can change over a lifetime.

What about "math class?" Is that a "phone" word? How about "math teacher," "curriculum," "assessment," and "Algebra 2" or "high school math?"

None of these are "phone" words. As a student in the 1930s and 1940s, my dad went to "math class" and learned from a "math teacher." Culturally and pedagogically speaking, how do you think his experiences compared with the experience of students in math classes today? Sure, it's changed in some ways—better technology and building codes have emerged, more girls and students of color have gained access to mathematics due to the feminist and civil rights movements. But fundamentally speaking, "math class" looks very much the same as it did almost a century ago. Our textbooks look much like they did before—even if they're online now. Students are assessed to make sure we—students, teachers, administration, school boards—are all held accountable to show improvement. And we still teach the same high school courses that we taught when "the Americans" were competing with "the Soviets" in the space race 60 years ago.

"Math class" is the opposite of a "phone" word. Changing our story about what "math class" is will require us to change a story we've been telling ourselves for a very long time.

> *Changing our story about what "math class" is will require us to change a story we've been telling ourselves for a very long time.*

Instead of spending time defining equity, I'd like us to start creating opportunities for us to be in each other's classrooms so we can create more shared lived experiences about what equity can look, sound, and feel like in math class. That's what we've been doing with words like "equity," "math class," and even "colleague" in our reflections, observations, and gatherings. I'm trying to change our meaning—our perception and conception—of these words, together, by inviting us to create more shared lived experiences with them. This is why we've been sitting in each other's classrooms and reflecting together on what we see. It's not about being right or wrong—it's about developing a shared common understanding while also fostering a shared appreciation for our differences.

Sometimes it's easier to create a new word we can define for ourselves. That's one of the fundamental purposes of the Island of Practice—to generate words with universal imagery that we can define together. It's sometimes easier this way because we don't have preconceived baggage around these words. We are calling it a Garden because I want to shed the cultural legacy we have with "math class" so that we can define it differently, together, for ourselves as a system of story making. The Tree—or whatever you call yours—creates a safer space for us to talk about our professional "identity" and "moral compass" and our "inherent biases." Those are not "sandwich" words—but a "Tree" is.

Equity Achieved Is an Unfinished Math Story of Flourishment

This is as far as I will go in terms of offering us a definition of equity: we are achieving equity when ALL of our students have a greater sense of confidence and an increased desire to keep their math story unfinished. Simply put, we've done our job well enough, if our students all want to keep learning more math when they leave our classrooms at the end of the year.

> We are achieving equity when ALL of our students have a greater sense of confidence and an increased desire to keep their math story unfinished.

I am inviting us to make that goal—to keep the math stories of our students healthy and unfinished—the Most Important Thing we value so that we can calibrate our actions and our measures in ways that enhance our students' identities and repair our broken cultural relationship with mathematics.

A powerful shift in our professional identity happens when we calibrate our work to focus on this Most Important Thing. We move away from seeing ourselves as teachers of content and move toward a mental model of teaching as a cultural act of keeping the individual and collective math story healthy, robust, and vibrant. Our goal becomes less about our students achieving mastery and more about the same goal that we've had for ourselves since the beginning of our journey—we want math class to foster our students' sense of mathematical *flourishment*. We want them to feel the same way about *learning* in math class as we do about *teaching* in math class.

Four Equity Actions That Have Emerged From Our Journey Together

The journey to furthering our expertise of achieving more equity in our classroom culture *starts with learning how to build equity for ourselves in our professional culture.* Look back on our learning together, and you will see what I mean. Everything we've done so far to build more equity into our culture of professionalism is about learning how to do the following:

- Position each other and ourselves as professionally capable.

- Enhance our professional identities in ways that foster our internal sense of agency.

- Elevate each other's voice—our individual and collective agency—in a culture where authority is shared.

- Value the multiple contributions we have to offer from our unique lived experiences.

These are the same actions (Figure 9.1) we must *further improve* with our students in our own classroom in order to build more equity in our classroom culture.

9.1 Four Equity Actions

1. Position our students, individually and collectively, as mathematically capable.

2. Enhance student identities in ways that foster their internal sense of agency.

3. Elevate student voices—their individual and collective agency—in a culture where authority is shared.

4. Value the multiple contributions our students have to offer from their unique lived experiences.

Note that the Four Equity Actions in Figure 9.1 are not new to the field of math education. They have been written about in dozens if not hundreds of books and journal articles for decades. They have become central tenets of organizations like NCSM and NCTM. It's a wonder we are still not seeing them lived out more broadly. In this book, these Four Equity Actions are simply a concise way to distill all the research language surrounding equity in a way that is useful to our journey.

I hope you see that you have a greater understanding of what equity means and that *we have a greater shared awareness of what equity feels like* because we've internalized these actions for ourselves, together. Now that we've learned how to elevate each other's voices, we are more capable of elevating the voices of our students. Now that we've learned how to enhance each other's identities and foster each other's sense of agency, we are more capable of doing these things with our students.

CONNECTING BACK TO ANNE AND CAROL

FOCUS

I invite you to recall the stories about Anne and Carol in Chapter 8 and to use the Four Equity Actions in Figure 9.1 as a lens to look through the window.

What evidence do you see of these Four Equity Actions in our planning session?

What evidence do you see of each of the Four Equity Actions in Anne's spontaneous instructional choices?

What missed opportunities do you see? How might we have done more? ●

What We Gain in a Story-Focused Garden

As we saw with The Group in Anne's classroom, the transition from a content-focused Garden to a story-focused one can be uncomfortable both for us and our students as we disrupt the long-standing cultural script about how math class is supposed to go. There will be hiccups. But we gain some empowering advantages when we do this. We've seen some already, but I would like to be explicit about a few that will be pertinent to our work moving forward.

Advantage 1: We gain an opportunity to create a shared lived experience of what equity looks, sounds, and feels like in a classroom. When we sit in on content-focused Gardens and talk about what we see, our discussions are often deficit-laden and focus on what content students "don't know" and what we need to do differently to "get them to learn" that content with different "instructional techniques." In a content-focused Garden, equity is often an afterthought—something we "add on" to our lesson plans after we've planned them. *OK, my lesson plan is complete. Now what about my language learners? And my students with IEPs? With ADHD? With emotional trauma and symptoms of PTSD?* In this mental model, equity risks becoming a checklist we simply try to complete. Equity also becomes something that we only do for the "marginalized"—sending tacit messages to our students that some need "equity" more than others.

Conversely, when we sit in story-based Gardens, we embrace a mental model of "math class" where our understanding of equity is in the foreground and is also more inclusive. Our discussions are more asset-based and *start with student identity and agency*—not just for those students who aren't experiencing success, but for all of our students.

We begin to think of our students more as the imperfect and unfinished human beings that they are rather than "standardizing" them and reducing them to a container we are trying to fill with "mathematics." We begin to embrace our natural state of humanity as caring people. With authority now shared more equally, we begin to build relationships that help each other find their own personal sense of flourishment with mathematics—the flourishment that is necessary to keep the story unfinished.

Advantage 2: We change the focus on what it means to be good at math. Making this shift helps us move away from answer getting and toward wondering, questioning, and understanding. Brilliance in math class becomes more inclusive to a wider diversity of learners. We become more aware of the academic biases in the room—systems and actions that position some students in ways that they are continually seen for their deficits and not for their brilliance. A story-focused math class is a math class that can work for all learners.

Advantage 3: We change how we think about why, what, and how we assess. In a story-focused Garden, traditional forms of assessments become less valuable because they are less useful. We begin to ask ourselves: *Who is this assessment for? If it's for our students, does it further their learning in ways that enhance their identity?* When we ask these questions, we begin to see that we cannot measure the things we value with traditional "tests" and "district assessments." In the absence of these methods, we create time and space to create, deliver, and assess math tasks in ways that further not just mathematical understanding but also the math stories of our students.

Advantage 4: We change student's relationship to learning. Here is where we get to the heart of what we gain out of this shift—relationships and all the flourishment that can come from them. In a story-focused classroom, the whole commodity exchange between us and our students becomes disrupted. The motivation for students to learn mathematics comes more from the inside—and less from us. We become more equal in our relationships with students because the authority of learning is shared with them. We create space to talk about, measure, and address the things we value most with our students—the vitality of their math story. We elevate student voice—individually and collectively—to hear what they value most and find ways to calibrate our teaching to those needs.

We have more leverage with these relationships in a story-focused Garden. Students trust us when we position them in ways that stretch their identity and challenge their sense of agency—they trust us because we've continually shown them that we believe they are capable, even in the face of failure. We create vantage for our students as they learn to see themselves and math class from a different perspective. Student-to-student relationships enhance as they stop looking to us as the authority in the room and begin to see themselves as active partners in each other's learning in class. And when mathematics becomes something they learn through each other, not from us, we know we are productively sharing authority.

It All Comes Back to the Headwinds and the Beacons

If you look closely at the language in Advantage 4 (about relationships), you will find language from the Beacons in there. The Beacons are not just guiding principles for our culture of professionalism with each other, but guiding principles for our culture in a story-focused Garden where authority is shared with our students.

I offer you the Headwinds and the Beacons again, this time written from the perspective of the student (Figure 9.2). What kind of story making is happening in your classroom? What would your students say about your math class?

9.2 **The Headwinds and the Beacons from the students' perspective**

The Headwinds (Student Edition) Story making in a content-focused Garden		The Beacons (Student Edition) Story making in a story-focused Garden
Efforts to improve my abilities in math class continue to come from the "top-down"—my teacher tries to make me learn.	→	The desire to expand my potential as a mathematical thinker comes from inside me.
I'm incentivized to value what my teacher measures and how it's measured.	→	I'm motivated in math class because the teacher measures things we value.
I operate in the silo of my own work space.	→	I must continually seek vantage on the thinking of my classmates and what they see from their perspective.
If you're not mathematically gifted, mathematics is something you learn by following a recipe of steps.	→	Mathematics is a craft we can study best through each other—even my teacher learns from me.

When we read the Headwinds from the students' perspective, we start to really understand why we have the cultural relationship with mathematics we do. Remember, the Headwinds are systemic. They don't just affect our professional development, they affect our curriculum, assessments, and all aspects of a "standardized math education"—including the math stories of our students. The learning we've internalized about how the system erodes our professional flourishment relates directly to the learning our students have internalized from years of math classes that have eroded their mathematical flourishment and diminished their math story.

To me, the Beacons in Figure 9.2 represent my "list of things I wish my students would say about my math class and their math identity at the end of the year." It is my vision of equity, and they symbolize my success criteria as a teacher of mathematics. I'm not suggesting that you use this language explicitly with your students, per se. I'm simply showing you that all of our learning through Parts 1, 2, and 3 is coherently connected. Everything we are learning to do for ourselves is what we need to help our students do for themselves.

> To me, the Beacons in Figure 9.2 represent my "list of things I wish my students would say about my math class and their math identity at the end of the year."

These Words May Not Be "Sandwich" Words, but They Must Become "Phone" Words

In Chapters 10 and 11, as we look at NCTM's Eight Math Teaching Practices through an equity lens, we will come across the following words and phrases:

Goals. Learning objectives. Tasks. Norms of participation. Position. Mathematical thinker (and doer). Just, equitable, and inclusive learning environments. Reasoning. Mathematical representations. Purposeful questions. Procedural fluency. Conceptual understanding. Elicit student thinking. Facilitate meaningful discourse. Productive struggle.

Like equity, these aren't exactly "sandwich" words—debating their definitions may be unproductive. But in order to make the shift to a story-focused Garden *together*, we must make them "phone" words. We must reach a shared understanding of what these words mean by having shared lived experiences with them. And the best way to do that with these words is to start being in each other's classrooms and talking about what we see.

KEY TAKEAWAYS FROM CHAPTER 9

* Equity is a concept with a meaning that we must let ourselves evolve on our journey of reflecting, calibrating, and collaborating. We must be willing to test our beliefs about our vision of equity and question the efficacy of the actions we are taking to achieve it.

* We must be in each other's classrooms so that we can move our learning beyond the definitions we are reading and start fostering a shared understanding of what equity can look, sound, and feel like in the classroom.

* When we make a shift from a content-focused Garden to a story-focused Garden, we start with equity as a core value behind all of our instructional choices. We seek to enhance their identity and foster their sense of agency in ways that further their math story.

* As stewards of our cultural math story, we are all trying to achieve the same Most Important Thing in our story-focused Gardens: provide our students with the flourishment they need to keep their math story empowering and unfinished.

INTERLUDE 9:
ACTIONS TO SHARE AUTHORITY

LIGHTHOUSE REFLECTION 6: REFLECT ON HOW AUTHORITY IS SHARED IN YOUR CLASSROOM

FOCUS

What does it mean to "share authority" in your own words?

What actions are you currently taking to share authority with your students?

Where is your expertise falling short? What does it look like in your Garden when you're not sharing authority?

What story making is resulting from how authority is shared?

Who answers student questions in the room? Are you positioned as the answer key and the authority of mathematics? Or are they positioned as being the answer key for each other?

How are cultural norms established in your classroom? Who enforces those cultural norms?

How are decisions for learning made in the classroom? Who decides when transitions are made? Who decides when assessments are given?

Actions to Share Authority in the Classroom

Below is a list of actions that you can take to share authority in your classroom and change how the authority for learning is shared. These are actions that can help you and your students navigate the cultural transition from a content-focused Garden to a story-focused Garden.

Peter Liljedahl's book *Building Thinking Classrooms* makes an excellent companion to *The Imperfect and Unfinished Math Teacher*. The first three actions on the list below can be found in his book and online. If you're looking for a deeper analysis of these actions (and others), I strongly encourage you to explore Liljedahl's highly effective suggestions for classroom practices that position learners as *thinkers* who are capable and share authority for learning in the classroom. In the online resources, I speak directly from my own experiences here having discovered these moves on my own.

- Defront the room.
- Use vertical nonpermanent surfaces.
- Use visibly random grouping.
- Normalize a process of seeking feedback from students.
- Record and analyze the words you use with students.
- Establish classroom norms *with* your students, not *for* your students. ●

 Further Your Craft: Learn more about these actions and download resources at bit.ly/3o7bBzq, or visit the The Imperfect and Unfinished *Math Teacher* Free Resources tab on the Corwin website. These actions are things you can deliberately observe in each other's math lessons during Seek Vantages and talk about in your Campfire Gatherings.

SEEK VANTAGE 6: WHAT MISSED OPPORTUNITIES DO YOU SEE?

VANTAGE

I invite you to choose one of the actions from the list above and commit to practicing it. You may choose the same one as a group or you can each focus on different ones. Regardless, spend time in each other's classrooms watching each other take deliberate actions to share authority with your students.

I also invite you to continue your informal huddles and ask yourselves:

What missed opportunities do you see?

What do you see? And how do you see it?

What might be some things I might want to consider from your vantage?

What do my students need right now?

What's going well right now?

How is the authority for learning shared?

Who is carrying the cognitive load right now? ●

CAMPFIRE GATHERING 6: AGENDAS TO FURTHER YOUR CRAFT OF SHARING AUTHORITY WITH STUDENTS

RELATIONSHIPS

In the Facilitation Guide for Campfire Gathering 6, you will find more details about the actions to share authority listed in Interlude 9. You will also find some suggested agenda activities that you and your colleagues can implement to help each other improve your expertise of sharing authority with your students. ●

NOTES

_____

_____

_____

_____

_____

_____

_____

_____

_____

_____

_____

_____

_____

_____

_____

_____

10

ESTABLISHING LEARNING OBJECTIVES IN A STORY-FOCUSED CLASSROOM

Where We've Been

In Chapter 9, I invited us to test this fundamental belief about our professional identity: we are not teachers of mathematical content so much as we are stewards of the math stories being authored by the students in our room. When we make this shift to a story-focused Garden, equity becomes embedded into our professional practice rather than something that is thought about as being separate and added on after the fact.

Where We're Going

In Chapter 10, we will look through two more windows together to examine, from the students' perspective, how we establish learning objectives in our classrooms. We will take a deep dive into this teaching practice and the research language that supports it as we continue to practice testing our beliefs by questioning our actions.

Classrooms that empower students to develop a strong sense of agency and that foster positive mathematical identities do so through a shared classroom authority. That is, students are positioned as having valuable knowledge to contribute to the classroom conversation, are given time to develop their ideas, and engage in meaningful discourse.

—NCTM, *Catalyzing Change in Middle School Mathematics* (2020b, p. 42)

Two Windows Into How Learning Objectives Can Be Established

We are about to enter two seventh grade classrooms and observe how two teachers establish the same mathematical goal to focus student learning. I invite you to suspend your judgments so you can view both experiences from the student perspective and think about the potential impact these teacher actions could have on the math stories being authored by students in each classroom.

WHAT MATH STORIES ARE BEING AUTHORED?

FOCUS

I invite you to recall Figure 9.2 from Chapter 9 that uses the Headwinds and the Beacons as a way to describe how math class is a story-making system from the students' perspective.

As you read, ask yourself, What potential math stories are being authored in each of these classrooms? What data are students seeing from their position? ✒

A Garden at the Headwinds School

Mr. Gale: *OK class. Our learning objective is up on the board. Let's all read it together.*

Half of the students (in chorus): *Today we will find the volume of cylinders to solve problems.*

Mr. Gale: *Let's do it again with full participation like the scholars we are.*

All students (in chorus): *Today we will find the volume of cylinders to solve problems.*

Mr. Gale: *That's better, thank you. Let's write this learning objective down in our math journals and get started on our notes today. Yesterday, we worked on finding the volume of prisms. Now we are going to build on that knowledge by learning to find the volume of cylinders. This lesson is a part of our geometry unit that we're working on as we study volume and surface area.*

A Garden at the Beacons School

Ms. Lux: *OK class. I have a story for you. When I was kid, my sister and I had this rule for when we had to share a soda: "You pour. I choose." One of us would get to split it up while the other one got to choose which portion they wanted. What were some of the ways that you had to share things with siblings or friends?*

Students share a few anecdotes, for example,

> On road trips, my sister and I have rules about who gets to sit in the front seat.

> My brothers and I have to share time playing video games.

> My friends and I share our snacks at lunch sometimes.

Ms. Lux: *Well, one time, my older sister did this to me. She poured the soda into two glasses like you see here in this picture I've got projected on the whiteboard. And I love soda, so I wanted the glass with more.*

Put yourself in my shoes. Which one do you think is more? How could you find out?

Students have 1 minute of quiet "think time" before they share in small groups. Then the teacher focuses the class for a whole-group discussion and charts some student responses for all to see on the

Photo courtesy of Dan Meyer

projected picture. In particular, she diagrams the dimensions and lists the key words that students seem to think are important.

After making their thinking visible, Ms. Lux pauses. *Let's take a step back and zoom out. How does this problem connect to what we've been learning in class lately? What's the same and what's different?*

Students identify that this problem is about volume, but these shapes are different. They're not like the prisms they've been looking at before. Circles are involved.

Ms. Lux: *Great start everyone. We're well on the way to understanding today's learning objective. We are going to extend our current understanding of volume by exploring these types of shapes more deeply and investigating how we can find their volumes. I'm going to ask that we're mindful today about sharing our thinking and listening to each other as we discuss some of the variables you've already suggested.*

FURTHER LEARNING

"You Pour, I Choose" is a task created by Dan Meyer. Check out similar tasks online by searching for "3-Act Math lessons" and the website 101qs.com.

Looking Through These Windows: How Is Authority for Learning Shared?

In terms of math content, both teachers have the same learning goal. But each of them have made choices about *how they establish their goals*—choices that have the potential to affect the math stories of our students in very different ways because they look, sound, and feel very different from the students' perspective.

The Potential Math Stories Being Authored at Headwinds School

On the surface, the action is efficient. The learning objective is established in less than a minute. *Let's get going!* It breaks down mathematics into a clearly defined and attainable skill. *Let's calculate the volume of cylinders!* It's made explicit in a way that is easy to measure. Teachers, and the administrators who hold them accountable, can easily cross it off the recipe checklist. *Is the learning objective explicitly written on the board and told to students?* Check. *Is the objective continually referred to in the lesson?* Check. *Is it assessed on an exit ticket?* Check. *Can it be easily measured on a Chapter Test?* Check.

Continued →

→ Continued

But let's look deeper and see what tacit messages may exist below the surface and the story making that is happening. When lesson objectives are established in the classroom like they are at the Headwinds School, learning in math class begins as a top-down, teacher-driven mandate that positions students as consumers of knowledge, not producers of it. Students are being told what they are learning and how they will learn it—without any room for their agency. *Read the objective. Write it down. Take notes.* These are all commands, softened only slightly by Mr. Gale's repeated use of the word "let's."

If teachers at Headwinds want students to see themselves as mathematical thinkers and to build up their sense of agency, then this method of establishing learning objectives may be an unproductive approach because it doesn't position students in a way that empowers them as learners. Instead, these actions generate data to students that implies the authority for learning in math class is all on the teacher. For teachers at Headwinds, their flourishment can become threatened because they may be engaging in actions that do not produce the student math stories they want.

Imagine the math stories students might author after several years of math classes where teachers regularly established mathematical goals as mandates of learning. How might that affect their math identity? If they were a student who, like me, thrived on taking notes, copying examples, and replicating those solutions on textbook problems in class, on homework, and on tests, their math identity might flourish in a Garden like this. But these students still risk not developing a robust sense of math agency because they come to expect that learning in math class is about learning whatever the teacher tells them to do. Mathematical knowledge remains something external, something that must be taught to them in "math class."

And what about students who need a different set of conditions to thrive? Perhaps this scripted and predictable opening of lessons, over time, turns them off to "math class," not because they aren't capable math people but because they don't feel included in this classroom environment. Perhaps they got tired of being treated as a passive consumer of learning—showing up every day and expected to be compliant to commands that *diminish* their math identities and *strip* them of their sense of agency. What actions would these students take in math class? What would be the interplay between their identity and their agency?

Some would likely withdraw from participating, put their heads down, and begin to give up. Some may exercise their agency in other ways—engaging in behavior that distracts, disrupts, or even sabotages the learning of others. And now we've potentially put ourselves in a position—a position we created through our expertise—of having to discipline students by exerting our authority over them. And we've all been there from time to time, right? It's a terribly unproductive position to try to author a productive math story—or find professional flourishment.

The Potential Math Stories Being Authored at Beacons School

By framing the lesson as an invitation for learning, math class begins immediately as a collaborative endeavor that has the potential to position students as being capable and competent. Through intentional storytelling and dialogue, the teacher is able to show students explicitly that their lived experiences have value in the classroom. By using a visual hook, the teacher is creating further opportunities for more students to have access to the mathematics of the lesson and to feel included. She offers quiet think time for students who may need the time to process their thinking internally before they're ready to listen to others. Because she invites her students to share their thinking about a situation, she's able to let the lesson objective emerge just as deliberately as Mr. Gale did, but in an organic way that shares the authority of learning with her students. She embraces spontaneity while also being intentional about her focus.

All this data is explicit to the students in the room. What's implicit is that when we make learning an invitation, we are saying tacitly to our students, *I share authority with you because you are capable. I elevate your voice because what you say is valuable. We are learners together in this math class.* We are not simply telling them they are capable—we are showing them.

Now, imagine the math stories students could potentially author after several years of math classes where teachers establish mathematical goals as invitations for learning. By making learning an invitation, they are developing a robust sense of agency. And by making learning inclusive, they are developing positive math identities. What actions would these students take in a math class? What would be the interplay between their identity and their agency?

My hunch is that most of them show up excited to learn because they know they are going to be valued, encouraged, and engaged in learning that doesn't bore them—*even if they don't think they're very good at math at the beginning of the year.* That's often what happens when

Continued →

→ *Continued*

> learning is always presented as an invitation—we put ourselves in a position to help our students author healthy and empowering math stories, no matter where their story is at. Our students are more likely to produce data that will nourish us, offering us the flourishment we need to remain imperfect and unfinished math teachers.

The Headwinds classroom is what can happen when we take a "content-focused" approach in our Gardens where the authority of learning is all on the teacher. The Beacons classroom is what can happen when we take a "story-focused" approach in our Gardens where the authority is shared with students. This is what happens when we think of ourselves less as teachers of mathematical content and more as agents engaged in the cultural work of positioning students so they author productive and unfinished math stories.

LANGUAGE NOTE

I'll be referencing these "Eight Effective Mathematics Teaching Practices" quite a bit in the next few chapters and will simply refer to them collectively as the 8EMTPs.

For the remainder of Chapter 10, we will do a deep dive into language behind the first of NCTM's (2014) Eight Effective Mathematics Teaching Practices as outlined in the *Principles to Actions* and expanded on in their *Catalyzing Change Series* for elementary, middle, and high school teachers (NCTM, 2018, 2020a, 2020b). These texts are rich with examples to further your learning and, with some simple internet research skills, you can find much of the content I'm referencing here on the NCTM website and elsewhere. I've also cited page numbers so you can go to these citations yourself.

Looking More Deeply Through These Windows: Getting at the "Whys" Beneath Our "Whats" and "Hows"

We all have learning objectives. Why? They're really important. Everything we do in the math classroom should have a focused objective. Even when our craft requires us to be spontaneous, we must be intentional about where we are going just as Ms. Lux did above and Anne did in Chapter 8. We also have learning objectives because the Headwinds make sure they're heavily embedded into our curriculum and assessments. But left to the Headwinds, *why* we establish our learning objectives often gets buried beneath unproductive beliefs about defining *what* a "good learning objective" is and *how* we go about establishing them "best."

Here are two definitions of what is meant when we say effective math teaching requires us to establish mathematics goals to focus learning (Figure 10.1).

10.1 Definition of "establish mathematics goals to focus student learning."

Effective teaching of mathematics establishes clear goals for the mathematics that students are learning, situates goals within learning progressions, and uses the goals to guide instructional decisions.
—NCTM, *Principles to Action* (2014, p. 10)

Mathematics learning goals should embody two components simultaneously: (1) The goals should identify the mathematical concepts, ideas, or strategies children will understand as a result of instruction; and (2) the goals describe the mathematical practices and processes [students] are learning to use to do the mathematical work.
—NCTM, *Catalyzing Change in Early Childhood and Elementary Mathematics* (2020a, p. 60)

Seems pretty obvious, right? We can't teach a lesson if we're not clear ourselves on the mathematical goals—the learning objectives—we want our students to learn. And we can't teach a unit of lessons if we don't clearly link these learning objectives in a coherent progression that makes sense to our students. And our learning objectives should focus on both the mathematics (what they will learn) and the mathematical practices students will embody (how they will learn).

We can read through these definitions and the research articles that support them, and we can sit in professional development and discuss our learning together, but as we learned in Chapter 9, discussing definitions and reading research articles only gets so far along our journey. We need a more focused understanding of the specific actions that embody this practice. Remember, one of the key components of deliberate practice is to focus on specific actions—not vague or general skills.

What are the actions? What does this EMTP look like?

Here are four specific teacher actions for this effective teaching practice. For readability, I've changed the verb tense to the active voice (Figure 10.2).

10.2 Productive actions that "establish mathematics goals to focus student learning."

> Establish clear goals that articulate the mathematics that students are learning as a result of instruction in a lesson, over a series of lessons, or throughout a unit.
>
> Identify how the goals fit within a mathematics learning progression.
>
> Discuss and refer to the mathematical purpose and goal of a lesson during instruction to ensure that students understand how the current work contributes to their learning.
>
> Use the mathematics goals to guide lesson planning and reflection and to make in-the-moment decisions during instruction.
> —*Principles to Action* (NCTM, 2014, p. 16)

These actions are clear, specific moves that we can—and should—deliberately practice in our classrooms. They are quite useful because we can support each other and hold ourselves accountable to furthering our expertise with these actions. But if we stop our *thinking* here, we risk reducing teaching down to a checklist. It is not sufficient for us to assume that just because we do these actions, we are creating a classroom that is inclusive for all the learners in it. We *may* be doing that, but the only way we know for sure is if we are willing to ask ourselves, "Are my actions creating the math stories I want my students to author?"

This is the primary difference you see between Mr. Gale's and Ms. Lux's classrooms. Both of them engage in these actions on the surface—they are compliant. But *how they do it* is different and so is the effect. Students in Mr. Gale's classroom are authoring math stories much different from those in Ms. Lux's because the teachers created vastly different lived experiences for their students. They *showed* their students very different things because they both have very different *whys* behind their actions. And this is where, in my opinion, the list of actions in Figure 10.2 can fall short—it doesn't get enough at our teaching *whys*.

What does this EMTP look like through an equity lens?

Deliberate practice requires us to focus on actions that *matter* to us—performance goals that we value because they are aligned to our vision of equity. Our work must yield flourishment or we won't be motivated. Left to the Headwinds, the language in the actions can become very *sterile*, almost clinical—there's no space for our own humanity in the language in Figure 10.2. It's not until we dive even further that we get to our "why"—the juicy stuff that matters to us most (Figure 10.3). (I've numbered them to help facilitate our conversation below.)

10.3 Looking at this Mathematics Teaching Practice through an equity lens.

> 1. Establish learning progressions that build students' mathematical understanding, increase their confidence, and support their mathematical identities as doers of mathematics.
>
> 2. Establish high expectations to ensure that each and every student has the opportunity to meet the mathematical goals.
>
> 3. Establish classroom norms for participation that position each and every student as a competent mathematics thinker.
>
> 4. Establish classroom environments that promote learning mathematics as just, equitable, and inclusive.
>
> —NCTM, *Catalyzing Change in Middle School Mathematics* (2020b, p. 59)

Now we're getting somewhere! These are actions we can not only use to calibrate our choices and hold ourselves accountable, these are actions that more readily align with our vision of equity. We're inherently *motivated* to achieve them. This is what "establishing mathematics goals" should *feel* like in a classroom environment where authority is shared. And this is the language I invite us to use as we begin to question our actions, individually and collectively, when it comes to how we establish our learning objectives.

If you're familiar with Simon Sinek's work, this language may sound familiar to you—changing a story always starts with the why. *Why are we doing this? Who is this action serving?*

When we start building our Garden with these initiatives in mind, we begin to build a system that encourages us to engage in "story-focused" teaching where the *whys* behind our actions are rooted in the student experience. Increase confidence. Support mathematical identity as a doer of mathematics. Norms of participation. Position each and every student as a competent mathematics thinker. Just, equitable, inclusive. *These aren't just the reasons why we establish mathematical goals. These are the reasons why we became teachers in the first place.*

FURTHER LEARNING

Simon Sinek has several 10- to 20-minute videos online. I find them worth the time, not just for what he has to say but also for how he moves the room as a storyteller.

A Deeper Look at Items 3 and 4

There's a *significant* amount of material in this single EMTP—too much to unpack here, but I would like to draw our attention to Items 3 and 4 from Figure 10.3.

▶ How do we *establish classroom norms for participation that more effectively position each and every student as a competent mathematics thinker and doer* (Item 3)?

▶ How do we *establish a classroom environment that does more to promote learning mathematics as just, equitable, and inclusive for all my learners* (Item 4)?

We'll return to these questions in the Interlude, but I invite you to come back to Items 3 and 4 throughout your careers by asking yourselves these same questions. I argue that if we could *excel at only two things* and it was *these two things,* we would heal our broken cultural relationship with mathematics in less than a generation.

A Deeper Look at Item 2

I want to take a moment to share my interpretation "high expectations" in Item 2 from Figure 10.3, because we may have a different vantage on the meaning of the phrase. I think we often misinterpret this to say, "we must hold our students to high expectations when it comes to meeting the mathematical goals we set for them."

The high expectations are not on our students here, *they are on us.* We must do our utmost to ensure that we have created equitable opportunities for each and every student in the room so they all have shared access to the learning process. It means that we hold ourselves to high expectations when it comes to using our teaching expertise to *show* each and every one of our students that they are mathematically competent and capable—regardless of the story they are already telling themselves about "math class" and who they are as "math people."

This is how we change their story—by showing them they are capable.

These "high expectations" require us to stop saying things like, *You were supposed to learn this last year. Why don't you know this already? You're not ready for this class.* I invite you to consider how students hear these words and how they might incorporate them into their existing math story. Potentially, they feel seen for their deficits. They potentially feel like you're blaming their previous teacher or maybe even them. How safe, welcomed, and included would these students feel in this classroom environment? How safe, welcomed, and included would teachers feel in this professional environment?

As I mentioned in Chapter 9, there will be very few times that I will ask us to *outright stop* doing something, and this is another one of those times. Can we please stop blaming our students for the position they are in? It's not their fault. Nor is it ours. The system puts our students in their position and it puts us in ours. *But it is on us to do something about it.* It's on us to make a new story for our students by testing what we know and questioning what we do and why we do it.

It doesn't matter how much we tell ourselves that we believe our students are capable. *We are all producing data that shows them that they are not.* Even with the best of intentions, our actions send tacit messages to our students—showing some of them that they are not capable, that math class is not for them. I ask that we all accept responsibility for this premise: *If a student believes that they are not capable at math, it's because that's what their lived experience has taught them—not because that's what we told them, but that's what we showed them.*

I'm not calling us out for something I haven't already called myself out for. One of the takeaways from the Rudy Story is that I blamed students *way too often* for the position they were in, and it took me *way too long* to see it. *It's important to know how your students see you, Chase.*

Breakthroughs in Performance Happen Suddenly

Before we move forward, I want to tell you something. Gale and Lux *are the same teacher.* This teacher made the shift in their professional identity—they began thinking of themself less as a teacher of content and more as a steward of math stories. Once this small shift in belief was made, *massive shifts* manifested in their classroom culture as the relationships with their students changed.

It only took *two weeks* for Gale to turn into Lux—the transition from a content-focused to a story-focused Garden didn't happen overnight, but it happened really quickly. The first few times didn't go that well. Students didn't know how to act—they expected to be told what to do. They were reluctant at first, and the teacher was discouraged. But over just a short period of time, with patience and persistence and grace, this teacher began to shift the math stories that were being authored in the room.

That's one of the key facts about deliberate practice and Ericsson's research—expert performers go long stretches with minimal improvement until a breakthrough emerges. It's a natural, albeit frustrating, reality of expertise. Here's the thing to remember—breakthroughs always come, and we never know when one is around the corner. And to find that breakthrough more efficiently, we must continually seek vantage on our beliefs and actions.

Last, I invite you to remember that changing a story is hard work and uncomfortable work—it takes energy and reflective thinking to step out of our confirmation biases and learn how to do something differently. The human brain is reluctant to change the stories it's telling itself. When we ask our students to change the stories they are telling themselves, we must remember that this is uncomfortable work for them too. We must learn to see their behavior as a reflection of their identity—and give them the grace they need along their journey.

KEY TAKEAWAYS FROM CHAPTER 10

* Math class isn't just where we teach content to students—it's a story-making machine. It is where a math story is authored.

* It's important to get past the *what* and the *how* so we can begin to look at our *why*. This is where our planning should start in a story-focused classroom.

* We must establish classroom norms for participation that position each of our students as mathematically capable. And we must create an inclusive classroom environment that promotes fairness, justice, and equity.

* We must stop blaming our students for the position they are in. It is on us to change the story by testing our own beliefs and questioning our actions by continually asking ourselves: *Is the story I am telling myself true?*

* Changing a story is hard work and can be uncomfortable. But significant breakthroughs can happen suddenly and significant shifts in our classrooms can occur quite quickly.

INTERLUDE 10: ACTIONS TO KEEP MATH STORIES UNFINISHED

LIGHTHOUSE REFLECTION 7: FOCUSING ON ITEMS 2, 3, AND 4

FOCUS

Some of your students will always come in with gaps in their understanding—their math stories will always be imperfect. And some of your students will always come in with damaged math stories—they don't identify as being capable learners and act accordingly. Our job is to do something about it so that their math stories stay unfinished. I invite you to continue to reflect and make sure that you are holding yourselves to high expectations to ensure that each and every student has the opportunity to meet the mathematical goals.

When you look at your Dump, ask yourself honestly the following:

- Am I blaming them for their deficits and seeing them only for what they can't do? Or am I positioning them in ways that I can elevate the brilliance I see in them?

- Can I do more to foster classroom norms for participation that effectively position each and every student as a competent mathematics thinker and doer?

- Can I do more to create a classroom environment that promotes learning mathematics as just, equitable, and inclusive for all my learners?

These aren't really "sandwich" questions. Answering them authentically will require a lot of vulnerability. Give yourself grace. And when it comes to sharing your responses in Mirroring Conversations, make sure you're giving each other the grace we need so we can be authentic and courageous. ●

SEEK VANTAGE 7: ESTABLISHING LEARNING OBJECTIVES

VANTAGE

I invite you to reflect on how you establish learning objectives in your lessons and examine your actions from the students' perspective.

Ask yourselves, do our actions

● position our students, individually and collectively, as mathematically capable?

● enhance student identity in ways that foster their internal sense of agency?

● elevate student voice in a culture where authority is shared?

● value the unique lived experience and the multiple contributions our students have to offer?

What story making is happening as a result of our choices establishing our learning objectives? What actions might be more productive to achieving your vision of equity? ●

CAMPFIRE GATHERING 7: AGENDAS TO FURTHER YOUR CRAFT OF KEEPING MATH STORIES UNFINISHED

RELATIONSHIPS

In the Facilitation Guide for Campfire Gathering 7, you will find some suggested agenda activities that you and your colleagues can implement to help each other improve your expertise of the Four Equity Actions (Figure 9.1) and Items 2, 3, and 4 (Figure 10.3) in ways that keep the math stories of your students healthy and unfinished. You will also find some suggestions for furthering your learning and deepening your relationships moving forward. ●

Further Actions

The invitations below are not simple actions that we can take tomorrow in our classroom because I'm inviting us to rise up against some of the most formidable Immovable Mountains on our landscape: curriculum, grading, and high school math content standards.

Ensure that all feedback we give students productively furthers their story. If your assessment doesn't further student learning, then I ask that you stop giving it. I've seen countless teachers undo weeks of culture building because they feel compelled to give a "chapter test" so that they can give students a "grade" for what they "know." Once we put a grade on a test, learning stops. That test goes in a binder or in the trash can on the way out the door. As an alternative to giving grades on assessments, consider giving every student feedback on where they can improve and spend the next day having them work together to further their learning. Show them that we value their mistakes as a part of the learning process.

When it comes to grades, teach students how to assess themselves. At the end of 12 years of math class, I had a binder with thousands of pages filled with tens of thousands of math problems that someone else showed me how to do. My hunch is that you have a very similar binder to mine. The only way we change that story is if we give fewer quizzes and tests and more tasks and rich problems in our classrooms. I know that tasks are more difficult to grade, *but that's not our job.* You don't need to grade their work, you just need to give them feedback that motivates them to do more thinking. Remember, our role is to further their learning—to keep their math story unfinished. That's always been our fundamental job—the spontaneous act of giving feedback that furthers learning for our students.

At the end of every month or so, I invite us to ask students to choose one task from that month and to reflect on it in ways that deliberately extend their learning. And throughout the year, we continually ask our students to curate and reflect on artifacts of their own learning. All of these artifacts are imperfect and unfinished because they are filled with our feedback and their revisions. And at the end of the year, they compile those tasks into a portfolio, and for their final, they use these tasks to tell us about their math story for the year in a style of presentation that honors their individuality.

As for the grades? If we stopped giving them, our classrooms will adjust and thrive. The system will freak out. We must hold ourselves to high expectations when it comes to showing evidence that all of our students are learning and thriving. It's essential that our students can *show* the system that our story-focused Garden is productively enhancing their math identity and abilities. And when that inevitable time comes when your position in this system mandates that a letter grade go on a "report card," I invite you to show your students how to do something that we've been learning how to do for ourselves throughout our journey—the ability to self-assess accurately and honestly. It's an essential skill for being a highly effective human being. Let's empower them to learn it.

I encourage us to use a textbook that is free. There are a few robust and wonderful textbooks that are online, *and they are completely free.* With your teacher email address, you can access full curriculum resources—printable student pages, well-crafted lesson plans, practice problems, performance tasks, and a variety of assessment options. Can we please spend less money on textbooks we don't need to buy so we can invest those resources into funding the pupil-free time we need to improve our teaching?

A few years ago, I got to witness a "state adoption process." It was as if the system created an event for itself just to reassure its own ego that it was still necessary. The "crappy textbook" in this story is what The District used. I promise you: this happened.

Who's All This for, Anyway?

For weeks, dozens of publishers and their employees spend millions of dollars and countless hours making sure their textbooks are compliant to The Checklist that The State says we need to meet in order to get our Stamp of Approval. This Stamp is *very* important to publishers. If you don't get it, your textbook isn't on The List, and schools can't use state funding to buy your textbook. For a small, nonprofit like us, not getting The Stamp would be a death sentence.

To determine if a textbook deserves The Stamp, more than a hundred well-intentioned, hard-working teachers, professors, administrators, and other math professionals gather, on The State's behalf, to meet with these publishers and evaluate their textbooks using The Checklist. These educators have also spent time in the weeks prior getting trained on The Checklist and learning how to use it to evaluate our textbooks. An ungodly amount of human-work-hours have gone into this adoption process.

The experts are divided into panels of about eight or so, and each of the publishers get assigned to a panel and our own conference room. One of the publishers in the same room with us makes a "crappy textbook." They've been working really hard the past two days to convince the panel that their curriculum deserves The Stamp, but there are some people on the panel who have some strong reservations. In particular, there's a man, a math Professor, who is deeply troubled by the nature of the crappy curriculum. *There's no mathematical thinking being done by the students here. Every lesson is a scaffolded walkthrough that sucks all the joy out of mathematics.*

By the time for the final vote, most on the panel acquiesced to vote for the crappy curriculum, but not the Professor. He held to his convictions.

The Leader of the Panel: *If you don't vote to approve this, then this curriculum won't get The Stamp.* This would be a stunning development—to see a leading publisher have their popular curriculum get snubbed.

Professor: *I can't in good conscience vote for this.*

I appreciated his courage and empathized with his plight. Our team had done our best to write a story-focused textbook we were proud of. We were one of the first to pass The Checklist. We were also aware of how *massive* and *influential* these large corporations were. They had *sway.* And the Professor, through no fault of his own, was caught in a position being pressed between his convictions and the Headwinds.

After some back and forth, Leader of Panel: *You don't have to vote for it. You can abstain from voting if you'd like. Would that ease your conscience knowing you didn't vote for it?*

Finally, the Professor relented to the sway. He abstained. I don't blame him one bit for not voting "no." But I realized that this whole "state adoption process" is absolute nonsense.

I doubt I was the only one asking myself, silently: *Who's all this for, anyway?*

De-linearize high school mathematics. I've avoided talking about high school mathematics because there's so much wrong with it. So much of the content we currently call "high school math" is unnecessary. It's remained relatively unchanged *for generations*. And its sole function seems to be a giant sorting machine determining who is a "math person" and "who isn't." I'm so mad about it, I wrote this book, and I will let the Rudy Story and the other stories speak for my beliefs here. High school mathematics finishes too many math stories and is destroying our cultural relationship with mathematics.

If I had a wish, I wish we could make high school math course offerings look more like college course offerings so we can "de-linearize" mathematics—it's NOT a linear field of study. Treating it as such actually *creates* much of the equity issues that we face. We must step out of the "Alg-Geo-Alg2 with a side of Stats" model to high school mathematics so that we can invite other rich mathematical ideas into our course offerings to students. There is absolutely no reason why we are wasting our humanity teaching students how to solve quadratic equations, prove endless theorems, and divide polynomials instead of, say, the mathematics of voting systems, apportionment, gerrymandering; statistics and the ability to know when they're being lied to; graph theory and other topics in discrete mathematics; mathematical modeling of real-world data using technology—you know, stuff that matters to our democracy these days.

MORE EQUITY ACTIONS FOR THE STORY-FOCUSED CLASSROOM

Where We've Been

In Chapter 10, we learned to see math class as a complex system of story making. Using one of the 8EMTPs, we looked through two windows into how authority can be shared in our classrooms when we establish our learning objectives.

Where We're Going

In Chapter 11, we will reinforce and extend our understanding of equity by seeing that, when you look at the 8EMTPs through an equity lens long enough, you realize all the language is interconnected and interrelated because it is all trying to express one single ineffable thing. What that ineffable thing means to you is up to you. I share what it means to me at the end of this chapter.

We do not live alone. We have never lived alone. We live in a world of extraordinary interdependence.

—Senge, "Systems Thinking for a Better World" (2014, 6:45)

Equity: It's All One Mobius Strip of Language

Nobody writes a book alone, and many have helped me along the way, but this book doesn't happen without my "co-thinking relationship" with Jeff Crawford. He's an imperfect and unfinished math teacher too, and Jeff continues to be an active partner in my professional growth as we deliberately reflect, calibrate, and collaborate on each other's thinking.

A Conversation With Jeff

One day, Jeff sent me a pic of this doodle he made.

Jeff: *What do you think?*

Me: *I see that you're thinking about equity actions. Tell me more.*

Jeff: *That "crosswalk" between the eight Effective Math Teaching Practices and equitable teaching practices has been on my mind a lot lately. After another great session with some Washington State Math Fellows, these three principles keep coming to the surface for me. I've been trying them out and they seem to be solid guides that help determine and clarify the action I would take or others might take for effective, equitable teaching.*

Photo courtesy of Jeff Crawford

Me: *You've been geeking out! I see an empty box. What's up with that?*

Jeff: *The empty box? What do others think? Is there something I'm missing? I'm not saying the list is perfect or complete and I want to keep pursuing it with others. I already have changes to my late night scribbles.*

Me: *What are you thinking of changing?*

Jeff: *When I say "position as capable," I really mean "position each learner as capable." Likewise, "enhance the identity and agency of each learner." Keeping the focus on each learner—each student, each educator, each parent, each community member—helps me remember that every single human being is worthy of being the center of learning.*

Me: *Love it. Hey, what's a "crosswalk" by the way?*

Jeff did two things for me that day. First, he created some vantage for me about some struggles I had been facing in my own efforts to describe equity. All the equity language, to me, kept folding in on itself—like it is all trying to describe some single "ineffable thing," just in different ways. To this day, when I look at the 8EMTPs through an equity lens and pull on one strand, I end up pulling on all the others. And if I keep going, I end up back to where I started—as if this language was all one rolling mobius strip—finite, but without boundary.

Second, Jeff reacquainted me with a table that aligned—crosswalked—the 8EMTPs with NCTM's own equity language. I had seen it a while before, yet had forgotten about it, and it ended up being the key document that I needed to bring focus to our final chapter.

A Crosswalk of Specific Equity Actions

The crosswalk shown in Figure 11.1 examines each of the 8EMTPs through an equity lens. To be clear, each of the items in the crosswalk are specific equity actions that you can take. Any of these actions has the potential to change the math stories your students are authoring and make math class work for more of your students. And as we saw in the stories of Anne and Carol or Mr. Gale/Ms. Lux, it is astonishing what big payoffs even a relatively small change can make. Before reading, I invite you to recall the window into Anne's classroom from Chapter 8 with the Numberless Word Problem that led to Miguel's 100 apples question. I've placed an asterisk (*) next to the actions we saw in our planning and teaching that day.

11.1 A crosswalk of equitable teaching practices

> This crosswalk is meant to spark conversations regarding intentional steps that can be taken ... to implement the eight Mathematics Teaching Practices in the most equitable ways and to represent some of the key ideas described ... by researchers in mathematics education.
> —NCTM, *Catalyzing Change in Middle School Mathematics*
> (2020b, pp. 58-61)

Establish mathematics goals to focus student learning. Effective teaching of mathematics establishes clear goals for the mathematics that students are learning, situates goals within learning progressions, and uses the goals to guide instructional decisions.	Establish learning progressions that build students' mathematical understanding, increase their confidence, and support their mathematical identities as doers of mathematics. Establish high expectations to ensure that each and every student has the opportunity to meet the mathematical goals.* Establish classroom norms for participation that position each and every student as a competent mathematics thinker.* Establish classroom environments that promote learning mathematics as just, equitable, and inclusive.*
Implement tasks that promote reasoning and problem solving. Effective teaching of mathematics engages students in solving and discussing tasks that promote mathematical reasoning and problem solving and allow multiple entry points and varied solution strategies.	Engage students in tasks that provide multiple pathways for success and that require reasoning, problem solving, and modeling, thus enhancing each student's mathematical identity and sense of agency.* Engage students in tasks that are culturally relevant. Engage students in tasks that allow them to draw on their funds of knowledge (i.e., the resources that students bring to the classroom, including their home, cultural, and language experiences).*
Use and connect mathematical representations. Effective teaching of mathematics engages students in making connections among mathematical representations to deep understanding of math concepts and procedures and to use as tools for problem solving.	Use multiple representations so that students draw on multiple resources of knowledge to position them as competent. Use multiple representations to draw on knowledge and experiences related to resources that students bring to mathematics (culture, contexts, and experiences). Use multiple representations to promote the creation and discussion of unique mathematical representations to position students as mathematically competent.*
Facilitate meaningful mathematical discourse. Effective teaching of mathematics facilitates discourse among students to build shared understanding of mathematical ideas by analyzing and comparing student approaches and arguments.	Use discourse to elicit students' ideas and strategies and create space for students to interact with peers to value multiple contributions and diminish hierarchical status among students (i.e., perceptions of differences in smartness and ability to participate).* Use discourse to attend to ways in which students position one another as capable or not capable of doing mathematics. Make discourse an expected and natural part of mathematical thinking and reasoning, providing students with the space and confidence to ask questions that enhance their own mathematical learning.* Use discourse as a means to disrupt structures and language that marginalize students.

Pose purposeful questions. Effective teaching of mathematics uses purposeful questions to assess and advance students' reasoning and sense making about important mathematical ideas and relationships.	Pose purposeful questions and then listen to and understand students' thinking to signal to students that their thinking is valued and makes sense.*
	Pose purposeful questions to assign competence to students. Verbally mark students' ideas as interesting or identify an important aspect of students' strategies to position them as competent.*
	Be mindful of the fact that the questions that a teacher asks a student and how the teacher follows up on the student's response can support the student's development of a positive mathematical identity and sense of agency as a thinker and doer of mathematics.*
Build procedural fluency from conceptual understanding. Effective teaching of mathematics builds fluency with procedures on a foundation of conceptual understanding so that students, over time, become skillful in using procedures flexibly as they solve contextual and mathematical problems.	Connect conceptual understanding with procedural fluency to help students make sense of the mathematics and develop a positive disposition toward mathematics.
	Connect conceptual understanding with procedural fluency to reduce mathematical anxiety and position students as mathematical knowers and doers.*
	Connect conceptual understanding with procedural fluency to provide students with a wider range of options for entering a task and building mathematical meaning.*
Support productive struggle in learning mathematics. Effective teaching of mathematics consistently provides students, individually and collectively, with opportunities and supports to engage in productive struggle as they grapple with mathematical ideas and relationships.	Allow time for students to engage with mathematical ideas to support perseverance and identity development.*
	Hold high expectations, while offering just enough support and scaffolding to facilitate student progress on challenging work, to communicate caring and confidence in students.
Elicit and use evidence of student thinking. Effective teaching of mathematics uses evidence of student thinking to assess progress toward mathematical understanding and to adjust instruction continually in ways that support and extend learning.	Elicit student thinking and make use of it during a lesson to send positive messages about students' mathematical identities.*
	Make student thinking public, and then choose to elevate a student to a more prominent position in the discussion by identifying his or her idea as worth exploring, to cultivate a positive mathematical identity.*
	Promote a classroom culture in which mistakes and errors are viewed as important reasoning opportunities to encourage a wider range of students to engage in mathematical discussion with their peers and the teacher.

CONNECTING TO YOUR OWN STORY

FOCUS

I invite you to reread these specific equity actions again. As you read, ask yourself:

> What language stands out to you as being the most important? How would you distill the essence of these equity actions in a shortened list like Jeff and I have tried to do?

> Which of these actions resonate most strongly with you and might offer you the most flourishment? Which of these actions might be a focus for you as you expand your potential? ●

Looking Through the Window: The Story-Focused Classroom

I can't create windows for each of the 8EMTPs. This book would be longer than a book you'd want to read and use. It's also unnecessary, because all of the 8EMTPs are naturally present, interconnected, and interrelated in a story-focused Garden. Creating windows for each practice would create the illusion that these teaching practices exist in a silo, separate from each other. We risk creating the tacit belief that these actions are all independent things, *but they are not*. They are all a part of the same thing—making math class just, equitable, and inclusive—or whatever language you use in your vision of equity.

As we look through the window from Chapter 8, we see that our choices that day can be, to some degree, described by all of these equity actions. In the planning session, we heard Anne and Carol talk about the high expectations they had for themselves to be able to create classroom spaces where all students have a chance to engage in the math task. They are discouraged by the "answer-shouting" behavior they are seeing in their classroom because they know that it excludes some students from participating.

Anne and Carol took actions to change the story of math class by implementing a task that had multiple pathways for success. Success in math class wasn't about getting the right answer. Instead, by creating an information gap, all students were positioned as competent mathematical thinkers as they explored a problem together. Three clear solution strategies emerged: solving division problems by adding up, solving division problems by subtracting down, and using ratio tables and number sense. All of these strategies ended in the same solution—more than 33 but less than 34. The remainder becomes a compelling and perplexing concept to talk about. These conceptual approaches to thinking about division lowered the math anxiety in the room as students were positioned as capable mathematical doers.

We didn't see this explicitly in Anne's lesson, but she's positioned herself to be able to select student work samples and begin her next lesson by comparing the multiple representations to create discussion. Anne and Carol elicited students' ideas by changing the textbook task into a Numberless Word Problem. Anne's actions in the lesson created space for students to interact with each other in ways that diminished hierarchical status among students.

When we examine the questions that were intentionally crafted and the questions Anne spontaneously asks, we see evidence of posing purposeful questions in ways that she can show her students that their thinking is valued. We see her pause as she deliberates on her response to Miguel's question and the other students' desire to solve the 100 apples problem. She's aware that her response will affect their math identity and sense of agency, and, to her credit, she vulnerably expresses a "not knowing" mindset in front of her students as we huddle in the back of her classroom.

She decides that Miguel's question is a task worth exploring and invites them to choose the problem they want to solve. *What do we have to lose? Why not turn them loose and let them struggle with it?* We see her consider the needs of students who might have a more productive learning experience solving the original question using manipulatives. We see her deliberately ask Miguel questions about his thinking and hear her celebrate his ideas. We see Miguel's positive mathematical identity when he's beaming walking out of his classroom—so much so that he tells his mother about it that afternoon.

How do I know he told his mom? That evening, after my day with Anne and Carol, I attended a function at the Headwinds High School, one of The District's "Back to School Nights" that they held throughout the year. I met a woman named Brenda. She had grown up in town and was a graduate herself of Headwinds High. She's a chef now, and she's just told me that she's not a math person.

Our Journey Returns to Where We Started

And it hasn't bothered me until recently. My daughter Page is in seventh grade now, and I get anxious when I help her with her homework. She's falling behind. Because of her low test scores, she has to go to intervention after school, and she feels dumb. I just don't want her to end up like me, hating math. I want her to feel empowered in the challenges she's going to face. But I don't know how to help her.

I also have a son. He's in third grade now—and that's the year they start taking the standardized tests. He's so capable and curious when it comes to numbers, but I see him becoming dulled by math class. Today was different for him though. He was all smiles when he came home. Apparently something happened in math class—something about Ms. Anne letting them do some middle school math?

I don't know. I'm just relieved that he found some joy in math class again. I lost my joy for it long ago, and it breaks my heart to see my daughter losing hers too.

I hope it's a different story for my Miguel. What do you think will happen to his joy for math in the years to come?

We Are All a Part of One Story

At the beginning of this chapter, I suggested that this equity language is all connected like one big mobius strip trying to express a single ineffable thing. To understand what I think of that single ineffable thing, I invite you to read through the Four Equity Actions shown in Figure 11.2. This time I have replaced the word "student" with "each other."

11.2 Four equity actions for humanity

1. Position each other, individually and collectively, as capable.

2. Enhance each other's identities in ways that foster their internal sense of agency.

3. Elevate each other's voices in a culture where authority is shared.

4. Value the multiple contributions each other have to offer from their unique lived experiences.

Framed in this language, the Four Equity Actions could also be "Four Parenting Actions to Raise Independent and Empowered Children" or "Four Ways to Help Other People Become More Fulfilled in Their Lives" or, my favorite, "Four Ways to Further Our Humanity."

To me, the intent of the equity language is to serve as a manual for how best to humanize one another—to position ourselves so we *continually* see that our well-being is interconnected and that our actions are interrelated. They remind us to give more than take, to elevate another's voice before we seek to elevate our own and to level unjust hierarchies that oppress others—*because we are all a part of one story.*

If we worked in a system that was equitable, would we have equity language? Perhaps. As I've mentioned, we are all biased about our own beliefs and what brilliance looks like in the math classroom. And equity language can help us test our own beliefs and question our own actions—the things we need to do to expose our biases that we don't yet see. And equity language can help us calibrate our actions in a story-focused Garden.

But we also have equity language *because the Headwinds make it necessary.* We are a loving species seeking to thrive in a system that dehumanizes us and our students by destroying our ability to relate to each other in more humanizing ways.

In my humble opinion, equity is what makes us a loving species.

KEY TAKEAWAYS FROM CHAPTER 11

* To me, the equity language is all connected. Pull on one strand, and you end up pulling on the others. I've defined them with my Four Equity Actions—actions that help remind us how to be a loving species as we navigate the Headwinds.

* The crosswalk (Figure 11.1) lists specific actions that you can take to achieve more productive and equitable outcomes in your classrooms. Grounded in equity language, these actions can be a launching point for you to further your teaching craft with deliberate practice.

INTERLUDE 11:
THE JOURNEY AHEAD

You *are* this universe. And you are creating. At every moment.

—Watts, *It Starts Now* (2020, 1:30)

Remaining Imperfect and Unfinished

Throughout our journey, I have invited you to think about the things you used to believe about effective math teaching, but no longer do and what it took to change your mind. And more important, I'm continuously inviting you to *intentionally put yourself in positions that will help you change your mind sooner.*

Throughout your career as an imperfect and unfinished teacher of mathematics, these are the components that will help you position yourselves—and each other—to see what unproductive beliefs and actions interfere with your ability to achieve more productive and equitable outcomes. These actions help us reflect, calibrate, and collaborate together as active partners in each other's professional growth.

- *Focus* and deeply reflect on the things you value most.
- Actively *seek vantage* from the student perspective to calibrate your actions.
- Build trusting *relationships* with others to help you see what you cannot see yourself.

When it comes to making new learning—and incorporating that new learning into our practice—we *must* be willing to ask ourselves a vulnerable question: *What if I'm wrong about what I believe and what I'm doing?* It may seem antithetical at first that we would find wholeness by asking ourselves a question rooted in such divisive language, but this question is at the heart of deliberate practice and forms the foundation of a "not-knowing" mindset. To get better at our craft, we must be willing to interrogate our mental models that may be preventing us from furthering our expertise. I share the stories in this book because I want to show you how important—and how difficult—it can be to create the vantage we need to create for ourselves. The Art of Not Knowing is uncomfortable work—it requires a lot of vulnerability and a lot of grace. And I hope I have modeled that level of vulnerability for you and shown you how capable we are at offering each other the grace we need to be imperfect and unfinished.

SUSTAINING FLOURISHMENT WITH DELIBERATE PRACTICE

FOCUS

At this juncture, you have many actions to help you further your craft and more fully achieve your vision of equity. Anne and Ms. Lux's classrooms offer us a window into how we can embody the equity actions in the crosswalk (Figure 11.1). More actions have been offered in the Interludes throughout Part 3. Now it's time to continue to engage in a regular habit of deliberate practice that focuses on expanding our expertise in these actions.

All the items in the crosswalk (Figure 11.1) are specific equity actions that you can deliberately practice. In the months ahead, I invite you to focus on the actions that give you the most flourishment as you continue to strive to improve your craft. I invite you to resist the temptation to quit if a new action doesn't go well at first. Keep at it and remember that breakthroughs in performance can happen suddenly.

Remember that once an acceptable level of performance is reached, growth stops. I invite you to keep pushing yourself to do better, to keep yourself on the edge of your comfort zone when it comes to flipping the script in your classroom with these actions. ●

I invite us to continue shifting our vantage by extending our practice of seeing math class from multiple student perspectives. Consider

VANTAGE

● teaching each other's students so you can create space for you to see your own students learn mathematics from someone else.

● co-planning and co-teaching a lesson together and reflecting on what you see.

● working with a coach and conducting a more formal lesson study cycle.

Last, one of my deepest regrets as a high school math teacher is that I never spent time in elementary and middle school classrooms while I was teaching full-time. I would've learned so much and seen the myriad of ways that I could improve my craft. I strongly ask that you consider traveling to another school site and start looking at math classrooms at multiple grade levels. I promise you, we all have something to learn from each other. The experience will be profound. ●

I invite you to keep utilizing the Campfire Gathering Facilitation Guide to help further your ability to be effective windows and mirrors to each other. More important, I invite you to improve and add to the Facilitation Guide by sharing your learning with us.

RELATIONSHIPS

- How might we improve the agendas in Part 2? What more could be done to make those prompts more useful to us? What prompts could we add?

- What other listening strategies and discourse activities could be added to our toolbox in addition to the ones offered here?

- What more could be added (or taken away) to make the facilitation of these agendas more feasible for you?

Creating a Grassroots Movement

Is it possible to embody our best insights about teaching and learning in a social movement that might revitalize education?

—Palmer, *Courage to Teach* (1998, p. 163)

This book is about to finish, but our journey—our story together—is very much *unfinished*. As a writer, I would consider myself successful if this book became well-worn with much use over the months to come. Write in it. Fold the corners of the pages. Come back to the stories, questions, and the invitations to actions. Keep learning to read it with new eyes. Make this book better by sharing your own story about being an imperfect and unfinished teacher of mathematics. You are an author too, just as much as I am.

I hope that you consider inviting others on this journey as you keep taking this journey yourself. Share your learning with others and be open to having your mind changed by them. As we spread the word about our empowering and rewarding culture of professionalism, I hope that more and more teachers of mathematics will find more flourishment in their work. And as more of us begin to embody a story-focused mindset toward our teaching, we will begin to repair and rehabilitate our cultural relationship with mathematics because we have succeeded in keeping the math stories of our students fulfilling enough that they remain unfinished.

EPILOGUE: FURTHER STILL

We must be willing to let go of the life we planned so as to have the life that is waiting for us.

−Joseph Campbell

In the true spirit of an epilogue, I would like to speak directly to you so that I may extend one more invitation: let's teach math class together, and afterward, let's break bread together and share stories about the things we've seen.

This has been my calling for some time.

In 2005, I woke up one morning, gripped by a vision of driving around the country in a converted school bus, meeting math teachers in their classrooms and learning from them. I remember a voice telling me: *There's people doing this math teaching stuff better than you are, Chase. Go find them. Learn from their stories. And share what you learn with others.*

The whole thing was absurd. *Who's gonna listen to a guy living out of a bus? How could I possibly create this cultural change in math education? I'm just an imperfect math teacher, with a bachelor's degree in English Literature, no less!* But that's the thing about callings—they come from a place we've yet to understand about ourselves, beckon us to places we don't know exist, and ask us to be someone we don't even know we are yet. To follow a calling is to surrender to the Art of Not Knowing.

For all of us, life in the pandemic forced us to reflect, take stock of the things that matter most to us, and prioritize how we want to best spend our time. I found myself being called by that voice again. *If not now, Chase, when?*

So in November 2020, I moved into a 17-foot U-Haul box truck that was converted into a tiny home. Not quite a converted school bus, but pretty close. I made this move, in part, to cut living costs so I could create more time to write this book. Most of these pages were written while living out of my box truck—parked on my dad's farm in Oregon taking care of elderly parents, parked in the desert of Arizona living in a community of artists and thinkers, and through the kindness of one of my favorite humans, parked on some private land in the beautiful mountains of Southern California for the final writing stretch.

The truck is named Grace, and she carries me wherever I go. She also carries something else, and it's important to this story.

Prior to this move, I lived in Venice, California. My backdoor was on a busy sidewalk—just off of Abbot Kinney at the corner of Andalusia and Cabrillo, if you happen to know the neighborhood. One of my favorite things to do in Venice was to sit on my back stoop, alone or with friends, and engage with people. It was an ideal setting to hear from a rich diversity of voices—people from all over the planet would walk by.

To call it a stoop is a bit of a stretch. It was just one step, barely big enough for two people. I would set out a table and a chair or two and invite passersby to share their thoughts on a prompt written on a whiteboard or chalk. *Who was your favorite math teacher—and why? How many ways can you solve 111 - 97? What's your math story? Tell me about your favorite number . . .*

Over time, I began to appreciate these conversations for continually reminding me of some important truths about our humanity. We instinctively seek opportunities for relationships—even if it's a short conversation with a stranger—because we long for the nourishing sense of belonging we feel when our story is shared, heard, and appreciated. And I believe that we all crave to give that nourishing sense of belonging to others by hearing and appreciating their story. The stoop is a place where we have a chance to embody our human need for belonging—to pause, connect, and engage with each other in authentic conversation; to listen to each other's stories; and to practice the courage to share our own.

We all need more "stoop sessions" in our lives—moments when we can exercise our humanity with each other and offer each other laughter, grace, and a good long hug. With this in mind, I've designed my tiny home on the back of Grace to be a sort of "Traveling Stoop"—I invite you to be a part of our stories. You can find us @TheTravelingStoop.

I don't pretend to know the next steps on our journey. The stoop is my own social experiment—my own lesson in the Art of Not Knowing. It's in this spirit of our humanity that I extend my invitation into your math classrooms and into your story.

I hope to see you down the road.

REFERENCES

Boaler, J. (2019). *Limitless minds: The new science that unlocks the mind and potential.* HarperOne.

Bruner, J. S. (1996). *The culture of education.* Harvard University Press. http://mehrmohammadi.ir/wp-content/uploads/2020/07/The-Culture-of-Education-Jerome-Bruner.pdf

Ericsson, A., & Pool, R. (2017). *Peak: Secrets from the new science of expertise.* Houghton Mifflin Harcourt. https://media.oiipdf.com/pdf/f83ba83f-4544-42c7-a944-e05982b0fccc.pdf

Green, E. (2014). *Building a better teacher.* W. W. Norton.

Herbel-Eisenmann, B., & Breyfogle, L. M. (2005). Questioning our patterns of questions. *Mathematics Teaching in the Middle School, 10*(9), 484–489. https://doi.org/10.5951/MTMS.10.9.0484

hooks, b. (2013). *Teaching community: A pedagogy of hope.* Taylor & Francis.

Klate, O. (1995). *Even on the wind: Selected poems, November 1992-December 1994.* Jonathan Klate & Carlotta Willis. (Original work published 1977)

Leinwand, S. (2019). *Blunt observations and practical strategies for orchestrating far more impactful PD in math* [Webinar]. Global Math Department. https://www.bigmarker.com/GlobalMathDept/Blunt-Observations-and-Practical-Strategies-for-Orchestrating-Far-More-Impactful-PD-in-Mathematics

Liljedahl, P. (2020). *Building thinking classrooms.* Corwin Press.

Margaret Wheatley. (2002, December 1). In *Wikiquotes.* https://en.wikiquote.org/w/index.php?title=Margaret_Wheatley&oldid=2899094

National Council of Teachers of Mathematics. (2014). *Principles to actions: Ensuring mathematical success for all.*

National Council of Teachers of Mathematics. (2018). *Catalyzing change in high school mathematics: Initiating critical conversations.*

National Council of Teachers of Mathematics. (2020a). *Catalyzing change in early childhood and elementary mathematics: Initiating critical conversations.*

National Council of Teachers of Mathematics. (2020b). *Catalyzing change in middle school mathematics: Initiating critical conversations.*

National School Faculty Reform. (n.d.). *Passion profiles.* https://www.nsrfharmony.org/wp-content/uploads/2017/10/passion_profiles.pdf

Palmer, P. J. (2008). *A hidden wholeness: The journey toward an undivided life.* Jossey-Bass.

Palmer, P. J. (2017). *The courage to teach: Exploring the inner landscape of a teacher's life.* Jossey-Bass.

Proust, M. (2003). *La Prisonnière* [The captive] (Vol. 5, Remembrance of Things Past, Trans. C. K. Scott Moncrieff). Project Gutenberg Australia. (Original work published 1923) https://gutenberg.net.au/ebooks03/0300501h.html

Senge, P. M. (2012). *Schools that learn: A fifth discipline fieldbook for educators, parents, and everyone who cares about education.* Crown Business.

Senge, P. M. (2014, December 15). *"Systems thinking for a better world"—Aalto Systems Forum 2014* [Video]. YouTube. https://www.youtube.com/watch?v=0QtQqZ6Q5-o

Smith, M., Bill, M., & Steele, M. D. (2020). *On-your-feet guide: Modifying mathematical tasks: Eight strategies to engage students in thinking and reasoning.* Corwin Press.

Stigler, J. W., & Hiebert, J. (1999). *The teaching gap: What educators can learn from the world's best teachers.* Free Press.

Stigler, J. W., & Hiebert, J. (2009). Closing the teaching gap. *Phi Delta Kappan, 91*(3), 32-37. https://doi.org/10.1177/003172170909100307

Typhoon. (2011). The honest truth. On *A new kind of house* [Album]. Oregon. https://genius.com/Typhoon-band-the-honest-truth-lyrics

Watts, A. (2013). *It starts now* [Video]. YouTube. https://www.youtube.com/watch?v=PfIYGaslVnA

Watts, A. (2020, November 23). *Waiting for magic* [Video]. YouTube. https://www.youtube.com/watch?v=WxoGX2oMPAE

INDEX

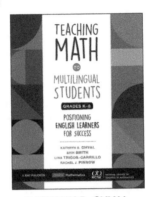
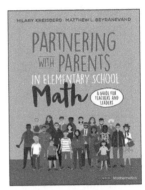

**JENNIFER M. BAY-WILLIAMS,
JOHN J. SANGIOVANNI, ROSALBA SERRANO,
SHERRI MARTINIE, JENNIFER SUH**

Because fluency is so much more
than basic facts and algorithms

Grades K–8

**KAREN S. KARP,
BARBARA J. DOUGHERTY,
SARAH B. BUSH**

A schoolwide solution for students'
mathematics success

Elementary, Middle School, High School

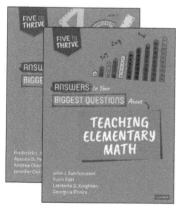

**JOHN J. SANGIOVANNI, SUSIE KATT,
LATRENDA D. KNIGHTEN, GEORGINA RIVERA,
FREDERICK L. DILLON, AYANNA D. PERRY,
ANDREA CHENG, JENNIFER OUTZS**

Actionable answers to your most
pressing questions about teaching
elementary and secondary math

Elementary, Secondary

**SARA DELANO MOORE,
KIMBERLY RIMBEY**

A journey toward making
manipulatives meaningful

Grades K–3, 4–8

CORWIN

A SAGE Publishing Company

Helping educators make the greatest impact

CORWIN HAS ONE MISSION: to enhance education through intentional professional learning.

We build long-term relationships with our authors, educators, clients, and associations who partner with us to develop and continuously improve the best evidence-based practices that establish and support lifelong learning.